I0235750

Notes to myself

and anybody else who might find them useful.

Written between

11/2022 and 11/2024

Edited and formatted between

11/2024 and 07/2025

TABLE OF CONTENTS

"A Stoic Resurrection: Notes from the Journal of a Modern Stoic"
© 2025 by Kontext & Satoshee Strategy
KONTEXT.EE / SATOSH.EE
ISBN: 978-0-473-75174-6
Licensed under CC BY 4.0. To view a copy of this license visit:
https://creativecommons.org/licenses/by/4.0/

1. On Love

ALL FOR LOVE & FREEDOM

///

WE ARE LEGION OF LOVE

///

ONLY THROUGH SACRIFICE
YOU CAN FIND LOVE.
(21.11.2022)

EVERYTHING DIES
WHEN IT'S NOT TAKEN CARE OF.
EVEN LOVE.
(24.11.2022)

"THERE IS ONLY LOVE"

THERE ARE NO COINCIDENCES.

THERE ARE ONLY CONSEQUENCES.

THERE IS NO LUCK.

THERE ARE ONLY PROBABILITIES.

THERE IS NO TALENT.

THERE IS ONLY PRACTICE.

THERE IS NO SEPARATION.

THERE IS ONLY UNITY.

THERE IS NO SUFFERING.

THERE IS ONLY LOVE.

(13.12.2022)

SELF LOVE IS NOT THE ANSWER.

LOVE FOR OTHERS IS THE ANSWER.

(24.12.2022)

SHE IS THE LIGHT.

SHE IS THE LOVE.

(12.02.2023)

I SUBSCRIBE TO NO RELIGION,
GURU, MENTOR,
OR NATION STATE.
MY RELIGION IS LOVE,
MY GURU IS MY HIGHER SELF,
MY MENTOR IS THE TAO
AND MY STATE IS FREEDOM.
(17.02.2023/07.10.2024)

THERE IS BUT ONE UNIVERSAL TRUTH,
AND THAT IS LOVE.
(11.03.2023)

TO SEE THE BEAUTY IN EVERYTHING IS
NOT THAT DIFFICULT.
ESPECIALLY IN THE UGLY THINGS.
BECAUSE THROUGH THE UGLY THINGS
WE LEARN.
AND BEAUTY IS LOVE IS GOD IS TRUTH IS
KNOWLEDGE.
(12.03.2023)

Real discipline, like real love, does not stem from rules. It stems from truths. Rules must be enforced, thus there is resistance and energy expenditure. Truths just are.

(13.03.2023)

Abstaining from pleasure or discarding pleasure is a fundamental flaw in one's philosophy or religion. If pleasure and desire were impure, they would not be associated with sex. But sex involves desire and is pleasurable, thus there is nothing inherently immoral or wrong in pursuing these things. It is only when we are disconnected from the truth, from love, is when we allow our minds to become vulnerable regarding questions of pleasure and desire.

(19.03.2023)

I AM BECOME LOVE,
THE CREATOR OF WORLDS.
OPPENHEIMER CHOSE
TO BECOME DEATH.
I CHOSE THE OPPOSITE.
(27.03.2023)

ONE OF THE MOST EVIL THINGS THE
SYSTEM HAS DONE IS THAT IT HAS
COMPLETELY SEPARATED THE IDEAS OF
SEX AND HAVING CHILDREN. SEX HAS
GONE FROM SOMETHING HOLY,
SOMETHING SACRED, TO SOMETHING
TRIVIAL. BY MAKING SEX TRIVIAL, IT HAS
BECOME MEANINGLESS. BY MAKING IT
MEANINGLESS, IT HAS MADE HAVING
CHILDREN MEANINGLESS. AND IF
CHILDREN ARE MEANINGLESS, THEN
EVERYTHING IS MEANINGLESS. BESIDES
OUR EGO, OF COURSE.
THEN, THE EGO CAN REIGN.
(02.04.2023)

WE'RE ALL GOING TO HAVE TO COMPETE
WITH AI. IN NEARLY EVERY POSSIBLE
FORM OF ENDEAVOUR. BUT WE WILL
ALWAYS HAVE THE ADVANTAGE
OF THE HUMAN TOUCH,
WHICH IS THE MIDAS TOUCH,
WHICH IS LOVE.
(05.05.2023)

SOMETIMES WE THINK ABOUT WHAT'S
THE MOST ROMANTIC THING WE COULD
DO TO WOO A CERTAIN SOMEBODY.
THE TRUTH IS, IF SHE'S INTO YOU,
ANYTHING YOU DO IS ROMANTIC.
IF NOT, THEN EVERYTHING YOU DO
IS CREEPY.
(29.05.2023)

IF THERE IS TRUE LOVE THEN I AM IT.
(20.06.2023)

LOVE WILL PREVAIL, THUS I CAN'T FAIL.
(23.06.2023)

TODAY IS A GREAT DAY TO:
PROCLAIM YOUR LOVE FOR THE WORLD.
(24.06.2023)

LOVE IS THE DEFAULT STATE. IT TAKES
NO EFFORT. FEAR, HATE, ANGER - THESE
ARE THE EMOTIONS THAT YOU MUST
CONSTANTLY FEED IN ORDER FOR THEM
TO EXIST. LETTING GO OF THOSE
EMOTIONS IS TO SIMPLY STOP FEEDING
THEM.
(24.08.2023)

MY LOVE FOR YOU IS UNDYING,
UNENDING, UNCONDITIONAL.
UNEXPLANATORY.
(29.08.2023)

IT'S NOT EASY BEING A HOPELESS
ROMANTIC IN A WORLD WHERE
ROMANCE IS DEAD.
MAYBE THAT'S WHY I'VE DECIDED TO BE
A HOPEFUL ROMANTIC INSTEAD :)
(21/23.09.2023)

WHICH DAILY ACTIONS, THOUGHTS
AND WORDS BRING ME CLOSER TO
LOVE AND FREEDOM?
(05.10.2023)

ALLOW YOURSELF TO BURN
THE FLAME OF LOVE.
(09.10.2023)

WHAT IS THE BEST WAY YOU CAN
EXPRESS YOUR LOVE TO THE WORLD?
(10.10.2023)

"IF THERE IS LOVE, THEN IT IS I" MEANS
THAT THE ONLY WAY TO EXPERIENCE
AND EXPRESS THE FEELING OF LOVE IS
THROUGH OURSELVES. THIS EARTHLY
EMBODIMENT. AND THIS, IN TURN,
MEANS THAT IF THERE IS LOVE THEN
YOU ARE IT. AND IF YOU ARE NOT IT, IF
YOU BELIEVE SUCH A THING DOES NOT
EXIST OR IS DEAD, WELL, I'VE GOT NEWS
FOR YOU MY FRIEND: IT'S YOU WHO IS
DEAD, WHO VIRTUALLY DOES NOT EXIST.
HOWEVER, AS LONG AS WE ARE HERE, IN
THIS PHYSICAL INCARNATION, WE CAN
REVIVE THAT PART OF US.
(26.10.2023)

ALL OF OUR ACTIONS ULTIMATELY STEM
FROM OUR NEED TO LOVE AND BELONG
IF WE COULD ALL ACKNOWLEDGE THAT
THAT WOULD BE GREAT
(01.11.2023)

CHAOS IS BORN OUT OF SCARCITY;
SUFFERING IS BORN OUT OF CHAOS;
STRENGTH IS BORN OUT OF SUFFERING;
ABUNDANCE IS BORN OUT OF
STRENGTH;
BEAUTY IS BORN OUT OF ABUNDANCE;
LOVE IS BORN OUT OF BEAUTY.
(08.11.2023)

SINCE EARLY AGE, WE HAVE BEEN TRAINED TO CONFORM. IN FACT, WE LOVE TO CONFORM DUE TO ONE OF OUR MOST INNATE NEEDS AS A SOCIALLY DEPENDENT SPECIES - THE NEED TO BELONG. TO RESIST THE URGE TO CONFORM YOU MUST CONTINUALLY REMIND YOURSELF OF THE FACT THAT ONLY BY BEING YOUR MOST AUTHENTIC, ORIGINAL SELF, CAN YOU FIND THE PEOPLE YOU REALLY BELONG WITH. OTHERWISE YOU JUST PLAY PRETEND, WHICH ALSO MEANS YOU PLAY PRETEND LOVE AND BELONGING.

(17.11.2023)

ULTIMATELY, WHAT YOU WANT FROM YOUR PARTNER IS FOR THEM TO SUBMIT TO YOU TO A DEGREE. YOU SHALL BE DEVOTED TO, AS IF TO A GOD, AND YOU SHALL DEVOTE YOURSELF, AS IF A HOLY PERSON. BUT, LIKE RELIGION, THIS CANNOT HAPPEN FORCEFULLY OR THROUGH DOCTRINES OR CONDITIONING. IT MUST BE ALLOWED TO HAPPEN, NATURALLY.

(10.12.2023)

JUST LIKE CRYING AND LAUGHTER "COME FROM THE SAME PLACE" I.E. ARE DIFFERENT EXPRESSIONS OF THE SAME PRIMORDIAL LIFE ENERGY, SO ARE LOVE AND GRIEF THE OPPOSITE EXPRESSIONS OF THE SAME CORE ASPECT OF THE HUMAN EXPERIENCE - THE FEELING OF UNITY, OF ONENESS, OF WHOLENESS (AND HOLINESS). OUR VERY CORE CONNECTION TO EVERYTHING ELSE. THIS IS, LITERALLY, WHY LOVE HURTS.

(15/20.12.2023)

A MANTRA:

"IF YOU DON'T DO THIS, NO ONE IS EVER GOING TO LOVE YOU."

REMEMBER THIS FUNDAMENTAL TRUTH ABOUT THE CONSEQUENCES OF THE FAILURES IN YOUR DUTIES AS A MAN. YES, YOU CAN USE IT TO HELP YOURSELF GET THROUGH YOUR EVERYDAY STRUGGLES. YOUR WORKOUTS. YOUR MENIAL TASKS. BUT WHAT THIS STATEMENT REALLY HAS TO PROPEL YOU TOWARDS IS YOUR HIGHER PURPOSE. YOU MUST FIND AND FULFILL THAT, OTHERWISE YOU WON'T LOVE YOURSELF. AND IF YOU DON'T, THEN NO ONE ELSE WILL, EITHER.
(26.01/19.05.2024)

How do you know when love is real? If that love genuinely makes you want to be a better person, then it's real. That's it. That's how you'll know.

(30.01.2024)

Love, gratitude, responsibility and empathy are the four fundamental qualities one should cultivate in themselves. All else will stem from there.

(04.02.2024)

Why do I do what I do? Well, why does anybody do anything? It's because we want to matter. We want to belong. We want to love and be loved. At the core of it, we are all very selfish creatures.

(11.02.2024)

IF THERE IS SUCH A THING AS LOVE, THEN IT IS YOU. LOVE IS AN ABSTRACT, IMMEASURABLE CONCEPT WITH NO DEFINING PHYSICAL PROPERTIES. THE ONLY WAY IT EXISTS IS THROUGH US; THE WAY WE PERCEIVE AND FEEL LIFE, OURSELVES, THE PEOPLE, AND IN FACT, THE WHOLE WORLD AROUND US. SO THE ONLY WAY FOR IT TO REALLY THRIVE IS FOR EACH AND EVERY ONE OF US TO EMBODY IT, TO LIVE IT. IT IS ONE OF THE HIGHEST POWERS AND IT CAN BE BROUGHT TO LIFE JUST BY THE VIRTUE OF YOUR THOUGHTS AND ACTIONS. BUT IT CAN ALSO BE DESTROYED AS EASILY. HERE'S THE FUN PART: YOU CAN REPLACE "LOVE" WITH ANY OTHER ABSTRACT, NON-PHYSICAL THING OR QUALITY SUCH AS: GOD, FEAR, TRUTH, HONESTY, SANTA CLAUS, ETC.

(12.02.2024)

GRIEF IS THE OPPOSITE OF LOVE -
AS IT IS LOVE WHICH FILLS YOU;
AND GRIEF WHICH HOLLOWS YOU.
APATHY IS THE OPPOSITE OF EMPATHY.
HATE IS THE OPPOSITE OF JOY.
(15.02.2024)

I CONSIDER "LOVE" AND "TRUTH" TO BE
SYNONYMS. HENCE, "LOVING YOURSELF"
DOESN'T NECESSARILY MEAN "BEING
NICE" TO YOURSELF. IT MEANS BEING
HONEST WITH YOURSELF.
(09.04.2024)

LOVE AND BELONG
ABOVE AND BEYOND
(15.05.2024)

You can't make anybody fall in love
with you.
They have to want to fall in love
with you.
(25.05.2024)

Love is God because love is the only
thing that can make us whole.
And to be whole -
is to live wholly, is to be holy.
It is that simple.
(12.06.2024)

I don't want to be a "player"
I want to be a *lover*
Cause in the end,
Players lose
And lovers win.
(26.05.2024)

People tend to view art and beauty as additions and auxiliaries to the pragmatic, rational, regimented, utility-focused "real life." I think it's the other way around. Materialistic and rigid "real life" only exists for us to be able to fully experience and appreciate the magic of poetry, of art, of beauty, of nature, of life itself. That's love. And that's what life's all about.

(03.07.2024)

There can be no life without love.
There can be no love
without trust.
There can be no trust
without truth.
Discard the pursuit of happiness.
Engage in the pursuit of truth.
For in truth, there is meaning
and in meaning, there is beauty.

(13.07.2024)

THERE'S THIS SAYING THAT HAPPINESS IS ONLY REAL WHEN IT'S SHARED. THAT'S NOT TRUE. YOU CAN BE IN COMPLETE SOLITUDE AND NOTICE A BEAUTIFUL BIRD, A FLOWER, A WILD ANIMAL OUT IN NATURE, OR A MEMORY MAY POP UP THAT ENTAILS IMMENSE HAPPINESS. AND YOU DON'T HAVE TO SHARE THAT EXPERIENCE OR FEELING WITH ANYONE WITHOUT IT BEING ANY LESS VALUABLE FOR IT. SOLITUDE IN AND OF ITSELF CAN BE A SOURCE OF HAPPINESS.

LOVE, HOWEVER...

IS ONLY REAL

WHEN IT'S SHARED.

(18.07.2024)

AFTER LISTENING TO A "WHAT IS MONEY"
PODCAST EPISODE IN WHICH ROBERT
EDWARD GRANT POSITED THAT JUDGMENT IS
THE OPPOSITE OF LOVE:

IF JUDGMENT IS THE OPPOSITE OF LOVE
AND I TEND TO SILENTLY JUDGE THE
PEOPLE AND THE WORLD AROUND ME,
WHILE BEING AFRAID OF BEING JUDGED
MYSELF, IS IT THEN ANY WONDER THAT I
KEEP FAILING AT LOVE? THAT I KEEP
FAILING AT INSPIRING LOVE, THAT I
KEEP FAILING AT MAKING ANYBODY FALL
IN LOVE WITH ME, INCLUDING MYSELF?
ALSO, IF ALL OF THE ABOVE IS CORRECT,
THEN THAT BEGS THE QUESTION: WHERE
DO YOU DRAW THE LINE BETWEEN AN
HONEST OBSERVATION AND JUDGMENT?

(21.07.2024)

IN ORDER TO TRULY LOVE AND BE
LOVED, YOU HAVE TO BE VULNERABLE.
IT'S BEING NAKED, ESSENTIALLY,
WHETHER LITERALLY, FIGURATIVELY, OR
BOTH. IN ORDER TO LOVE AS YOU
REALLY ARE, AND BE LOVED AS YOU
REALLY ARE, YOU HAVE TO TRUTHFULLY
BE AND EMBODY THAT WHICH YOU
REALLY ARE.

(12.10.2024)

*"THE DESIRE TO BE LOVED IS THE LAST
ILLUSION. GIVE IT UP AND YOU WILL BE
FREE."*

— MARGARET ATWOOD

WHAT ABOUT THE DESIRE TO LOVE? IS
THAT AN ILLUSION AS WELL? I THINK
NOT. I THINK THAT'S THE MOST
NATURAL THING OF THEM ALL.

(23.11.2024)

2. On Freedom

I DO EVERYTHING WITH FULL TRUST
IN MY OWN INTUITION, DRIVEN BY
THE IDEALS OF LOVE AND FREEDOM.
(11.11.2022)

CONDITIONING IS A SUBTLE WAY OF
FORCING.
(14.03.2023)

RESPONSIBILITY = ABILITY TO RESPOND
NOBILITY = ABILITY TO BE NOBLE
FITNESS = ABILITY TO ADAPT
FREEDOM = ABILITY TO ACT
(28.12.2023)

You cannot attain freedom without the grace of God. For as much as you seemingly can, you will be, in fact, shackled to your Earthly, sensory perceptions, desires and possessions. **True freedom is being free to be who you really are**, and it is a dream, dreamt by many, lived by few, as it is only the few who have the slightest clue to what that is. Let me make it clear that by the word "God" I don't mean God as is described in any particular religion, as I do believe all those descriptions are to a larger or lesser degree, inaccurate at best, or straight up deceptive at worst. Nor do I talk about a concept that is outside of, or separate from, ourselves. Rather, I would equate the word to "The Universe," "The Source," or, quite simply, "everything" as it is all-encompassing, omnipresent energy.

(21.01.2024)

Being free... is not as much about
being able to do what you want,
as it is about
being able to do what you need.
(21.01.2024)

I have been blessed by problems (i.e.
opportunities), uncertainty (i.e.
freedom), and the hubris (i.e.
stupidity), to think that I could
make some sense of it all.
(29.03.2024)

Don't know; doesn't matter.
(27.10.2023)

If you stay within your boundaries,
you're never going to expand them.
(29.10.2023)

You need to follow your intuition even more closely, more thoroughly, more intimately... Only do what feels right and is good. Remove the resistances and let the energy flow through freely.

(22.12.2023)

You know, you start with a blank sheet. Every day. Every day, it can be a new story. Life is an RPG.

(10.01.2024)

Travelling gives you constantly tons of ways to reinvent yourself. I've also realized that having a lot of uncertainty constantly in your life can vastly improve your ability to drown out the noise and focus on the present, the task at hand. It needs practice, sure. But it can also be highly beneficial.

(10.01.2024)

They say home is where the heart is.
Well, my heart is broken
into a million pieces,
dispersed across the globe.
(10.05.2024)

Karma's either a bitch or the
sweetest, most tender lover one
can ever have.
It's like, your choice, man.
(27.05.2024)

I hate the question
"what do you do for a living?"
I don't do anything for a living. I
do the living in order to do
whatever it is that I'm supposed to
do. What is that?
How would I know? If I knew it
I probably would have done it
by now.
(03.07.2024)

YOU ARE SO LUCKY. I KNOW IT'S HARD TO SEE IT THAT WAY WHEN YOU'RE IN THE MIDST OF THINGS. BUT YOU ARE. THINK OF ALL THE WONDERFUL PRIVILEGES YOU'VE HAD THROUGHOUT YOUR LIFE. THINK OF ALL THE WONDERFUL PRIVILEGES YOU HAVE RIGHT NOW. I MEAN, YOU HAVE SO MANY THAT QUITE OFTEN YOU FIND IT HARD TO CHOOSE ONE OVER THE OTHER! PERHAPS THAT'S ALSO WHY, FOR NOW, YOU HAVE BEEN UNABLE TO ACQUIRE AND UNLOCK EVEN MORE AND RARER TYPES OF PRIVILEGES. YOU HAVE TO HAVE CLARITY, BUT EVEN MORE IMPORTANTLY, YOU HAVE TO HAVE CONTROL OVER YOUR ENERGIES AND YOUR ATTENTION - THE WAY YOU DIRECT THEM IS PERHAPS THE BIGGEST FACTOR IN THE OUTCOME OF EVERYTHING IN YOUR LIFE.

(07.11.2024)

YOU HAVE TO INTERNALIZE
TO YOURSELF HOW MUCH FUN
THIS IS GOING TO BE.
HOW MUCH FREEDOM YOU HAVE
TO EXPRESS YOUR IDEAS
AND CREATIVITY.
(13.11.2024)

3. On Creativity

You don't hurt me.
You inspire me.
(December 2022)

What are you going to do
about it? Are you going to
get angry
or get creative?
(22.12.2022)

The only known cure
for the pain of existence
is the joy of creation.
(25.12.2022)

I WORK ALL THE TIME. EVEN WHEN I'M DOING "FUCK ALL," AS SOME WOULD DESCRIBE IT, LIKE SMOKING WEED AND JUST VIBING OUT TO MUSIC, I'M EXPERIENCING LIFE, I'M FEELING IT, RIGHT? AND MY "WORK," SO TO SPEAK, IS CREATIVE, IN LARGE PART. IN FACT, ALL WORK IS CREATIVE TO A DEGREE SINCE WE LITERALLY CREATE VALUE, WE SOLVE PROBLEMS BY DOING WORK. OF COURSE, SOME WORK ACTUALLY CREATES PROBLEMS BUT THAT'S A WHOLE OTHER DISCUSSION. AND WHERE DOES CREATIVITY STEM FROM? IT STEMS FROM THE EXPERIENCE, FROM LIFE ITSELF. SO, IN ESSENCE, ANYTHING THAT ENHANCES YOUR EXPERIENCE ENHANCES YOUR CREATIVITY ENHANCES YOUR PRODUCTIVITY. WORK AND PLAY MERGE INTO ONE AND THE SAME.

(17.01.2023)

SOUND IS AN EXTREMELY PURE FORM OF
CREATION. BECAUSE IN THE DIMENSION
OF SOUND, WE CAN CREATE PRETTY
MUCH ANYTHING FROM PRETTY MUCH
NOTHING.

(05.02.2023)

ANYTHING YOU CREATE YOU MUST GIVE
AWAY. IF YOU DEEM YOUR CREATION TO
BE BAD OR DESTRUCTIVE IN AND OF
ITSELF, IT MUST BE DESTROYED.
OTHERWISE, IT'S EXTRA WEIGHT ON
YOUR SHOULDERS.

(12.02.2023)

YOU ARE THE CREATOR.

(14.02.2023)

LIFE IS A DANCE. YOU CAN DANCE JUST FOR FUN. YOU CAN DANCE OVER, ABOVE AND BEYOND OBSTACLES. YOU CAN DANCE WITH YOUR EYES CLOSED. OR EYES OPEN. YOU CAN DANCE TO THE MUSIC OR IN COMPLETE SILENCE. YOU CAN DANCE BY YOURSELF OR WITH OTHERS. YOU CAN DANCE WITH A PARTNER. AND IF YOU'RE DANCING WITH THE RIGHT PERSON, AND YOU'RE GOOD AND CARING AND COMPASSIONATE, AND JUST A LITTLE BIT LUCKY, YOU MIGHT GET A KISS AT THE END OF THE DANCE.

(21.02.2023)

FIND YOUR INNER CHILD.

NURTURE HIM. LET HIS EXCITEMENT, THIRST FOR FUN AND KNOWLEDGE, AND HIS SHEER CAPABILITY TO LEARN AND UNLEARN GUIDE YOU.

BUT DO IT ALL WITH THE PROFICIENCY, EFFICIENCY, ACCURACY, COMPASSION AND POWER OF AN ADULT.

NO, NOT EVEN JUST AN "ADULT," THAT'S A VERY "AVERAGE" WAY OF LOOKING AT YOURSELF.

NO, NOT A MERE "ADULT," BUT A YOUNG GOD, A CREATOR, DEVELOPING HIS SKILLS AND HARNESSING ENERGIES.

(26.02.2023)

Since we are a direct representation of God on Earth, our most basic need and mission is to create. Ourselves, first and foremost, through self-preservation and reproduction. That's why these are the fundamental truths or rules of everything we can loosely categorize as animate.

Energy is God, since energy is the source of all creation, and God is the source of all creation, and to regain your energy is to regain your status as an integral and powerful part of it.

(11.03.2023)

PARENTS NEED TO PAY CLOSE
ATTENTION TO WHAT TYPES OF GAMES
THEIR CHILDREN ARE PLAYING. BECAUSE
THE TYPE OF THE GAME, COUPLED WITH
THE ABILITIES TO FOCUS ON THE GAME
AND THE CHILD'S INVENTIVENESS IN
COMING UP WITH THE GAME ARE A
HUGE INDICATOR OF HOW THEY ARE
GOING TO APPROACH LIFE AS THEY
GROW UP. THAT'S WHY IT'S SO
IMPORTANT TO GIVE CHILDREN THE
MEANS TO MAKE UP THEIR OWN GAMES
AND THEIR OWN STORIES WITHIN
THOSE GAMES, AND NOT FORCE THEM
TO JUST FOLLOW A SET OF RULES OR A
STORY. ONLY THEN CAN THEY FULLY
REALIZE THE POTENTIAL OF THEIR
IMAGINATION, AND PLAY THE SORTS OF
GAMES THEY TRULY WANT TO PLAY.

(09.04.2023)

I NEED PEOPLE TO INSPIRE ME.

I WANT TO LIFT PEOPLE UP AND ALLOW
FOR THEM TO LIFT ME UP AS WELL.

(19.06.2023)

I THINK A PROBLEM IN JOURNALISM,
MOVIES, AND ALL SORTS OF CREATIVE
CONTENT TODAY IS THAT IT MUST
"CHECK BOXES" INSTEAD OF BEING
ORIGINAL OR ACTUALLY INTERESTING.

(20.06.2023)

IF YOU CREATE CONTENT THAT CAN BE DIGITALLY DISTRIBUTED AND YOU CHARGE PEOPLE BEFORE ACCESSING YOUR CONTENT, THEN THAT TELLS ME THAT YOU ARE ACTUALLY UNCERTAIN IN THE VALUE OF YOUR WORK. WHY? BECAUSE IF YOU WERE CERTAIN THAT WHATEVER IT IS YOU ARE TRYING TO SELL HAD ANY SUBSTANTIAL WORTH, THEN YOU WOULD TRUST THESE PEOPLE TO PAY YOU IN ONE WAY OR THE OTHER, RETROACTIVELY. THE DISTINCTION BETWEEN PRICE AND VALUE IS, AGAIN, CRITICAL IN THIS FRAMEWORK BECAUSE, AS JEFF BOOTH SUCCINCTLY SAID: "PRICES FALL TO THE MARGINAL COST OF PRODUCTION" AND THE MARGINAL COST OF PRODUCTION FOR DIGITAL DATA IS ALREADY EFFECTIVELY ZERO AND IT IS GETTING EXPONENTIALLY CHEAPER AS WE SPEAK. THAT HAS NOTHING TO DO WITH THE VALUE OF THE VERY SAME DATA, THOUGH. PRICES ARE MERE AGREEMENTS. VALUE IS INNATE.

(17.07.2023)

"INFORMATIVE" IS ONLY A SECONDARY OBJECTIVE OF MY WRITING.

THE PRIMARY IS "INSPIRING."

AND YOU DON'T INSPIRE ANYONE WITH MEDIOCRITY.

(18.07.2023)

PEOPLE THINK THEY LIKE ORIGINALITY, BUT THEY DON'T. THEY LIKE TO HEAR SOMEBODY ELSE SAY WHAT THEY ALREADY THINK. THEY ARE LOOKING FOR REASSURANCE, NOT KNOWLEDGE.

I DON'T CATER FOR REASSURANCE.

(08.08.2023)

IF YOU ARE AN ARTIST WORRYING ABOUT AI "STEALING YOUR JOB," THEN YOU ARE PROBABLY NOT A VERY GOOD ARTIST :)

(17.08.2023)

YOU KNOW THIS THING, THIS THING
THAT'S SO BAD IT JUST SCREAMS AT YOU?
THERE YOU HAVE IT. THAT'S YOUR
CALLING.
(05.10.2023)

LIFE IS ART AND WE ARE ALL ARTISTS.
WE ARE ALL OUR OWN LITTLE
ENTERPRISES AND THUS, WE ARE ALL
ALSO ENTREPRENEURS.
(25.10.2023)

EVERYBODY INSPIRES ME. GREAT PEOPLE
INSPIRE ME TO BECOME MORE LIKE
THEM, TERRIBLE PEOPLE INSPIRE ME TO
BECOME LESS LIKE THEM.
(26.10.2023)

ANY ENERGY THAT'S NOT DIRECTED AT
CREATING ORDER WILL INVARIABLY BE
DIRECTED AT CREATING ENTROPY.
(28.12.2023)

Curiosity is the seed from which the tree of knowledge can emerge. However, a seed is unable to germinate on its own, in isolation. The conditions must be correct. The right soil with the right nutrients, adequate amounts of sunlight, moisture and warmth are all necessary for the process to take place. Similar conditions are required in humans for the tree of knowledge to grow and hopefully, one day, bear the fruits of intelligence. The requirement for curiosity to emerge in the first place is willingness to admit not knowing. The second requirement is the eagerness or need to know. Smash these 2 hard truths together like rocks, and you get the spark of curiosity, which, under the right conditions, can start a fiery passion.

(08.01.2024)

IF NOTHING INTERESTS YOU, THEN YOUR SOLE PURPOSE AUTOMATICALLY BECOMES TO FIND INSPIRATION.

(20.03.2024)

A TRUE ARTIST UNDERSTANDS THAT HIS CREATION IS NOT IN SERVICE OF HIM; BUT HE IS IN SERVICE OF HIS CREATION.

(28.05.2024)

SENSITIVITY, CREATIVITY AND FEMININITY ARE LIKE THIS COSMIC *MÉNAGE À TROIS* OUT OF WHICH THE PINNACLES OF ARTISTIC MASTERY ARE BORN.

(13.06.2024)

THE QUINTESSENTIAL EVIL OF THE
EDUCATION SYSTEM IS THAT IT DOES
NOT REWARD CREATIVITY, ORIGINALITY,
LEADERSHIP ABILITIES, PERSONAL
GROWTH, OR EVEN SOMETHING AS
BASIC AS ARGUMENTATION SKILLS.
INSTEAD, IT REWARDS CONFORMITY,
COMPLIANCE AND REGURGITATION
SKILLS, FIRST AND FOREMOST, AND ALAS,
THIS IS WHAT SOCIETY LOOKS LIKE.
(18.06.2024)

DON'T BE JEALOUS. DON'T BE ENVIOUS.
BE INSPIRED.
(07.08.2024)

COPYRIGHT LAWS ARE NOTHING ELSE
THAN AN IMPEDIMENT TO CREATIVITY
AND A GATEKEEPER TO KNOWLEDGE.
CHARGING MONEY FOR INFORMATION,
WHICH IN DIGITAL FORM IS NEAR-FREE
TO STORE AND TRANSFER, MIGHT AS
WELL BE CONSIDERED A FORM OF USURY.
(07.08.2024)

ALL WE DO IS SERVE AND PROTECT,
LEARN AND RESPECT.

(29.08.2024)

THE SUN IS SHINING, SO SHOULD YOU :)

(22.09.2024)

CYPHERPUNKS WRITE.

(25.09.2024)

YOU SHOULD BE WAKING UP EVERY DAY
WITH A SENSE OF WONDER AND
EXCITEMENT. THAT'S WHAT "THE LAST
DAY OF THE UNIVERSE" / "THE FIRST DAY
OF THE UNIVERSE" REPRESENTS.* THAT'S
HOW IT SHOULD BE APPROACHED.

IF IT'S NOT HAPPENING YOU SHOULD
FIGURE OUT WHY - AND SHIFT YOUR
PERSPECTIVE AND ACTIONS
ACCORDINGLY.

(29.09.2024)

* SEE MANTRA #6 (PAGE 251)

DON'T THINK ABOUT WHAT IT HAS
BEEN. THINK ABOUT WHAT IT CAN BE.
(08.11.2024)

1. I'M NOT ENTITLED TO ANYTHING
AND I'M GRATEFUL FOR EVERYTHING.
2. IT IS MY DUTY TO PUT WHATEVER I
GET INTO GOOD USE. WITHOUT
JUDGMENT. WITHOUT PREJUDICE.
AND THAT IS SOMETHING THAT I CAN
DO AND WILL DO. THAT IS A PROMISE.
(18.11.2024)

4. On Suffering

You have not accepted suffering. That is your problem.

(November 2022)

It is important to know and keep in mind that there will be sacrifice and with it, suffering, one way or another. You are sacrificing your time as you read or listen to this. Your attention. Your energy. Every day you go to work, you go to school, you work out, you take risks, you sacrifice *something*.

Even when you do nothing at all, you are sacrificing your time and even worse, you are sacrificing your *potential*.

(November 2022)

THERE WILL BE SUFFERING, YES.
BUT YOU GET TO PICK HOW YOU SUFFER
AND MORE IMPORTANTLY,
WHAT YOU SUFFER FOR.
(NOVEMBER 2022)

ANGER. APATHY. FEAR. THEY MUST ALL
BE OVERCOME IN ORDER TO REACH
ACCEPTANCE. ACCEPTANCE IS ALSO
SYMPATHY, WHICH IS ALSO HARMONY.
JIDDU KRISHNAMURTI SAID "HARMONY
IS STILLNESS." WHICH IS TRUE, BUT IT'S
ALSO UNTRUE, BECAUSE WHILE IT IS
STILLNESS, IT'S RELATIVE STILLNESS.
RELATIVE TO EVERYTHING ELSE AROUND
YOU, YOU'RE STILL. BUT THAT'S ONLY
BECAUSE YOU'RE IN TUNE WITH
EVERYTHING AND AS A COLLECTIVE
WHOLE, YOU'RE RESONATING,
VIBRATING. FOR THERE TO BE HARMONY
THERE HAS TO BE A MOVEMENT, A
FREQUENCY.
(29.05.2023)

THERE IS NO LIFE WITHOUT SUFFERING.
IF YOU DON'T CHOOSE WHAT TO SUFFER
FOR, THE DECISION WILL BE MADE FOR
YOU. SO. FUCKING. CHOOSE.

(07.09.2023)

SOMETIMES YOU HAVE TO TAKE THE
WRONG PATH IN ORDER TO REALIZE IT'S
THE WRONG PATH.

(21.09.2023)

I WOULDN'T BE TALKING ABOUT THE
LIGHT SO PASSIONATELY IF I HADN'T
SEEN, FELT AND EXPERIENCED THE
DARKNESS.

(21.10.2023)

YOUR CAPACITY TO SUFFER IS DIRECTLY
CORRELATED TO YOUR CAPACITY TO
LIVE.

(17.03.2024)

I KNOW YOU ARE ALONE. I KNOW YOU
ARE SUFFERING. THAT'S LIFE.

YOU HAVE TO:

1. ACCEPT THAT AS IT IS

2. REALIZE THAT EACH AND EVERY ONE
OF US HAS THEIR UNIQUE ABILITY, IN
SOME WAY, SHAPE OR FORM, TO REDUCE
THE AMOUNT OF SUFFERING INFLICTED
ON OTHERS

3. REALIZE THAT CONVERSELY, WE ALSO
HAVE THE ABILITY TO INCREASE THE
SUFFERING OF OTHERS, MAINLY
THROUGH THE MECHANISM OF OUR
MISGUIDED ATTEMPTS TO REDUCE OUR
OWN SUFFERING - MUCH OF WHICH
STEMS FROM THE MINDSETS OF
SCARCITY AND FEAR

4. REALIZE THAT ULTIMATELY, THE BEST
THING YOU CAN DO FOR THE WORLD,
AND YOUR SOUL, IS TO VOLUNTARILY
TAKE UPON YOURSELF AS MUCH OF THE
WORLD'S SUFFERING AS YOU POSSIBLY
CAN, WITHOUT BREAKING

IF YOU'RE STILL ALIVE, YOU AIN'T
BROKEN YET. EVEN IF YOU OR ANYBODY
ELSE IS TRYING TO CONVINCE YOU
OTHERWISE. AGAIN, I AM REMINDED OF
ONE OF MY FAVORITE QUOTES:

*"OUR LIVES ARE DEFINED BY THE
POSITIVE IMPACT WE HAVE ON OTHERS."*
— JEFF BOOTH
(22.04.2024)

SCARCITY IS BORN OUT OF WEAKNESS;
WEAKNESS IS BORN OUT OF
COMPLACENCY.
(MAY 2024)

I LEARNT THAT SUFFERING IS AN
INTEGRAL PART OF THE HUMAN
EXPERIENCE AND THAT MOST OF OUR
PROBLEMS STEM FROM TRYING TO
AVOID SUFFERING.
+ TO ADD TO THAT: MOST PEOPLE DON'T
HAVE ANYTHING TO SUFFER FOR.
SO THEY RESORT TO NARCISSISM.
(10.05.2024)

SACRIFICE IS TO MAKE SACRED.
(19.05.2024)

THE PATH TO GREATNESS IS THROUGH
SUFFERING.
(28.06.2024)

SUFFERING EXISTS EITHER WAY, I THINK.
LOVE IS WHAT GIVES IT MEANING, A
REASON, MAKES IT BEARABLE. IF THERE IS
LOVE, YOU CAN TRANSCEND SUFFERING.
(23.07.2024)

OH YOU'RE SCARED? GOOD. YOU
SHOULD BE SCARED, IF YOU'RE DOING
SOMETHING MEANINGFUL. BUT YOU
SHOULD REALLY BE SCARED OF NOT
BEING SCARED. THAT'S WHEN YOU'RE
BEING LULLED TO SLEEP. THAT'S WHEN
YOU'RE NOT BECOMING EVERYTHING
YOU COULD BE.

(11.08.2028)

WHATEVER YOU DO,

DON'T FEEL SORRY FOR YOURSELF.

(20.08.2024)

TIME FLIES WHEN YOU'RE HAVING FUN.
TIME CRAWLS WHEN YOU'RE SUFFERING.
THAT'S HOW YOU MANIPULATE TIME.
USE THAT AS YOU WILL.

(21.08.2024)

OFTEN, YOUR DETERMINATION TO
PURSUE SOMETHING NEW IS VERY MUCH
CORRELATED TO YOUR FRUSTRATION
WITH THE OLD.

(06.10.2024)

WHAT IF YOU'RE RIGHT
WHERE YOU NEED TO BE?
ISN'T THAT A SCARY THOUGHT?

(15.10.2024)

THIS MAY NOT BE WHAT YOU WANT.
BUT IT PROBABLY IS WHAT YOU NEED.

(19.10.2024)

YOU WILL FAIL. LOTS. BUT THROUGH
THEM YOU ALSO GET TO THE VICTORIES.

(07.11.2024)

LIFE IS SUFFERING. BUT IN ORDER TO
ASCEND THAT, YOU NEED TO SEE THE
BEAUTY AND THE LOVE BEYOND
SUFFERING. THAT'S WHAT MAKES IT
BEARABLE. THE MORE BEAUTY AND LOVE
YOU ARE ABLE TO SEE AND FEEL, THE
MORE BEARABLE IT BECOMES. THE
SUFFERING JUST IS. ONE WAY OR THE
OTHER. IT IS YOUR JOB TO MAKE
SOMETHING OUT OF IT.

(10.11.2024)

YEAH I GET IT. I GET IT WHY SHIT IS
STRESSING ME OUT. WHY IT BOTHERS
ME. IT ASKS ME TO DO SOMETHING
ABOUT IT. IT'S MY CALLING.

(18.11.2024)

5. On Enlightenment

CURIOSITY CREATES LUMINOSITY.

(17.11.2022)

TRUE WEALTH EMANATES FROM WITHIN.

(18.11.2022)

3 STEPS TO ENLIGHTENMENT:

1. REALIZE YOU USED TO SUCK

2. REALIZE YOU SUCK NOW

3. REALIZE YOU WILL SUCK IN THE FUTURE

(08.01.2023)

THE BEAUTIFUL THING ABOUT
SPIRITUALITY IS THAT IT'S VERY SIMPLE.
YOU DON'T HAVE TO READ A BOOK OR
FOLLOW ANY RULES OR LISTEN TO A
TEACHER. ALL YOU REALLY HAVE TO DO
IS UNLEARN, FORGET, LET GO OF
EVERYTHING. ALL YOU ASSUME IS TRUE,
ALL THE PRECONCEIVED NOTIONS.
ONCE YOU CAN DO THAT, EVERYTHING
ELSE WILL ARISE NATURALLY.

(04.03.2023)

NOT MIND OVER MATTER, BUT
MIND WITH THE MATTER.

(07.03.2023)

REAL ENLIGHTENMENT IS PROBABLY
WHAT HAPPENS AFTER DEATH.

(12.03.2023)

I THINK THROUGH CHILDREN IS
THE ONLY "REAL" WAY OF ACHIEVING
IMMORTALITY.

(12.03.2023)

ENLIGHTENMENT, SAMADHI, IS NOT
FULLY ATTAINABLE ON THE PHYSICAL
LEVEL. YOU CAN EXPERIENCE MOST OF
IT. BUT LIKE SOMEONE SAID, WHEN YOU
REACH ENLIGHTENMENT, YOU LITERALLY
TURN INTO LIGHT. PERHAPS THAT'S
WHAT AURAS ARE. THAT INNER ENERGY,
THAT ENLIGHTENMENT THAT EMANATES
FROM WITHIN.

(14.03.2023)

YES, IT'S LIFE AND DEATH. IT'S ALL LIFE
AND DEATH, BROTHER. BUT NOT IN A
MANIC, FEARFUL SENSE. IT'S ALL LIFE
AND DEATH IN THE SENSE THAT
EVERYTHING MATTERS.

(16.03.2023)

I HAVE BEEN EITHER LUCKY, OR SMART, OR DUMB ENOUGH NOT TO HAVE READ MANY BOOKS ABOUT "SPIRITUALITY" NOR TAKEN ANYBODY'S WORDS FOR THE ABSOLUTE TRUTH. BUT I'VE ALSO NEVER DISMISSED ANY IDEAS WITHOUT HEARING THE ARGUMENTS FOR THEM FIRST, AND THEN PAYING ATTENTION, TO MYSELF AND MY SURROUNDINGS, TO SEE IF THESE CLAIMS HAVE ANY VALIDITY IN THE REAL WORLD OR NOT.

(21.03.2023)

YOGA, FOR ME, IS A SCIENCE OF ENERGIES. FEELING, DIRECTING, HARNESSING ENERGIES, AND CHANGING THEM FROM ONE FORM TO ANOTHER. THESE ENERGIES EXIST ON ALL LAYERS OF REALITY AND YOGA SHOULD BE THE ART OF UNIFYING THESE DIFFERENT LAYERS INTO ONE COHESIVE FRAMEWORK.

(21.03.2023)

EGO DEATH IS NOT MERELY THE DEATH
OF THE EGO, IT'S THE REBIRTH OF THE
EGO. YOU WILL STILL BE YOU, AND YOU
WILL STILL HAVE AN EGO, ONLY THAT
NOW YOU WILL HAVE LEARNED ABOUT
THE UNDERLYING ONENESS OF
EVERYTHING. YOU WILL KNOW THAT
YOU CAN EASILY LET GO OF ANYTHING
ASSOCIATED WITH THAT EGO. AND YOU
WILL KNOW THAT YOUR EGO IS
PRECISELY WHAT ENABLES YOU TO BE
YOU, IT'S WHAT GIVES YOU YOUR
UNIQUE PERSPECTIVE AND SKILLSET TO
SERVE THE WORLD. SO YOU WILL REALIZE
THAT EGO IS NOT AN ENEMY, IN ANY
WAY. IT IS A CORE PART OF YOU AND
YOUR EXPERIENCE,

AND YOU WILL EMBRACE IT.

(12.05.2023)

IF A BLIND MAN CANNOT APPRECIATE
THE VALUE OF A FINE PAINTING, WHO'S
AT FAULT? THE BLIND MAN OR THE
PAINTER? NEITHER. IN REALITY,
HOWEVER, THERE ARE MANY BLIND MEN
WHO ARE BLIND SIMPLY BECAUSE THEY
CHOOSE TO KEEP THEIR EYES CLOSED.
(07.06.2023)

SPIRITUALITY IS SO STUNNINGLY SIMPLE.
IT'S WHAT HAPPENS WHEN WHAT YOU
HAVE TO DO AND WHAT YOU WANT TO
DO MERGE INTO ONE.
YOU CAN ALSO CALL IT "PASSION."
(12.06.2023)

I WOULD NEVER GO AS FAR AS TO CALL
MYSELF "AWAKE" OR "ENLIGHTENED." I
THINK THAT'S A SLIPPERY SLOPE. THERE'S
ALWAYS MORE TO BE LEARNED ABOUT
THE UNIVERSE, ABOUT YOURSELF.
(26.06.2023)

THE "AWAKENING" IS THE REALIZATION:
"IF WE DON'T PROVIDE ACTUAL VALUE
TO THE WORLD, WE'RE FUCKED."
AND IT IS HAPPENING ON ALL LEVELS:
INDIVIDUAL, COMMUNITY,
COMPANY, COUNTRY.
(01.07.2023)

I HAVE BEEN BLESSED.
EVERYBODY'S BEEN BLESSED.
MOST JUST DON'T FUCKING REALIZE IT.
(13.07.2023)

BEING AWARE OF, AND OKAY WITH,
DEATH, WHICH COULD ARRIVE AT ANY
SECOND, MAKES EVERY MOMENT THAT
MUCH MORE VALUABLE.
(27.07.2023)

LIVE EVERY DAY AS IF IT WERE YOUR
LAST, AND AS IF YOU LIVED FOREVER,
SIMULTANEOUSLY.

(29.07.2023)

"SPIRITUAL PEOPLE" WHO INSIST THAT
THEIR IDEA OF SPIRITUALITY IS THE
"RIGHT" ONE, ARE NOT
SPIRITUAL PEOPLE.

(19.08.2023)

WHAT IS LIFE? I DON'T KNOW, YOU JUST
TAKE CARE OF THINGS AND THINGS
WILL TAKE CARE OF YOU.

(05.10.2023)

IF YOU'RE AWARE OF IT,
YOU'RE IN CONTROL OF IT.
AWARENESS IS KEY.

(08.10.2023)

A SPIRITUAL MAN RECOGNIZES
THE DIVINE IN HIMSELF.
AN ENLIGHTENED MAN RECOGNIZES
THE DIVINE IN EVERYBODY ELSE.
(12.11.2023)

REMEMBER THIS: THE LIGHT CAN VERY
EASILY PENETRATE THE DARKNESS, BUT
DARKNESS CAN NEVER PENETRATE THE
LIGHT.
(23.11.2023)

WHAT IF EVERYTHING IS THE WAY IT IS
BECAUSE THAT'S THE WAY IT'S SUPPOSED
TO BE, YOU KNOW?
ISN'T THAT A SCARY IDEA?
(08.12.2023)

FOR I AM ALREADY DEAD;
EVERYTHING IS EXTRA.
FOR I AM ALREADY IMMORTAL;
EVERYTHING IS FOREVER.
FOR I AM ALREADY NOTHING;
EVERYTHING IS FOR GIVING.
(15/16.01.2024)

TRUE RELIGION IS POWER:
(GOD) ENERGY APPLIED
OVER (SPACE)TIME.
(11.02.2024)

BECOMING ENLIGHTENED IS NOT ONLY
ABOUT FOCUSING ON THE BRIGHT SIDE.
IT'S ABOUT ILLUMINATING THE DARK.
(14.05.2024)

WHO WOULD HAVE THOUGHT THAT
WE'D WALK AROUND WITH LITERAL
SUPERCOMPUTERS IN OUR HANDS, EACH
HAVING ACCESS TO BASICALLY THE
WHOLE OF THE LIBRARY OF ALEXANDRIA,
IF NOT MORE, YET REMAIN SO
UNENLIGHTENED? DARE I SAY
DEGENERATE EVEN, LOOKING AT
POPULAR CULTURE?

(16.05.2024)

AS A MAN, GETTING YOUR HEART
BROKEN BY SOMEONE YOU DEEPLY LOVE
CAN BE ONE OF THE BEST THINGS TO
EVER HAPPEN TO YOU. THE LIGHT WILL
ENTER THROUGH THE WOUND AND
ILLUMINATE THE PARTS OF YOU THAT
YOU NEED TO WORK ON. THE MOST
IMPORTANT THING IS TO NOT CONCEAL
THE WOUND I.E. TO KEEP YOUR HEART
OPEN.

OTHERWISE, THE WOUND WILL START ROTTING AND BEFORE YOU KNOW IT, YOUR WHOLE SOUL IS ROTTEN AND ALL YOU'LL BE LEFT WITH IS HATE AND RESENTMENT.

REALLY IT'S JUST ANOTHER FORM OF EGO DEATH. YOU HAVE BEEN SHATTERED INTO PIECES. NOW, YOU HAVE 2 CHOICES: YOU CAN EITHER TRY TO PRETEND AS IF YOU HAVEN'T, AND TRY TO HOLD THOSE PIECES IN PLACE, WHICH IS FUTILE, AS THE CRUMBS WILL TURN INTO DUST AND DISSIPATE THROUGH YOUR FINGERS. THE SECOND OPTION IS TO LET GO, LET THE PIECES FALL WHEREVER THEY WANT TO, RECUPERATE VIA PHYSICAL WORK/EXERCISE AND CONNECTION TO MOTHER NATURE, AND THEN REBUILD YOURSELF, ASSUMING A BETTER, STRONGER, MORE EFFICIENT FORM COMPARED TO WHAT YOU WERE BEFORE.

(18.05.2024)

THERE ARE NO NEGATIVE AND POSITIVE
THINGS. THERE ARE THINGS YOU CAN
CHANGE, AND THINGS YOU CAN'T.
THERE ARE THINGS THAT MOVE YOU
CLOSER TO THE TRUTH, TO GOD, TO
LOVE, AND THINGS THAT MOVE YOU
DEEPER INTO THE ILLUSION, THE MAYA,
THE MATRIX. UNDERSTANDING THESE
BASIC PRINCIPLES WILL GIVE YOU A
STARTING POSITION THAT'S BETTER
THAN WHAT 99.9% OF THE WORLD HAS.
"A STARTING POSITION FOR WHAT?"
YOU MAY ASK. LOOK AROUND YOU.

IT'S A BATTLE FOR YOUR SOUL.

(01.06.2024)

IN ORDER TO GET BETTER, THIS IS
EXACTLY WHAT YOU MUST DO:
YOU MUST CONFRONT THE PARTS OF
YOURSELF THAT FRIGHTEN YOU.
THEN THEY CAN BRIGHTEN YOU.

(09.06.2024)

LOVER WRITER FREEDOM FIGHTER
BUT ABOVE ALL,
A NOBODY.
(19.07.2024)

WHEN PEOPLE TALK ABOUT "BEING
GRATEFUL," THEY USUALLY TALK ABOUT
THE GOOD THINGS IN THEIR LIVES, THE
THINGS THEY'VE SUCCEEDED AT, THE
BEAUTIFUL MEMORIES THEY'VE AMASSED.
YES, WE SHOULD CERTAINLY BE
EXTREMELY GRATEFUL FOR ALL OF THAT.
BUT PERHAPS EVEN MORE SO, WE
SHOULD BE GRATEFUL FOR ALL OF OUR
FAILURES AND HARDSHIPS, BECAUSE
THESE ARE ULTIMATELY THE THINGS
THAT DRIVE US FORWARD, THAT REALLY
MAKE US GROW AS HUMAN BEINGS.
(04.08.2024)

EVERY MOMENT YOU'RE ALIVE IS A GIFT.
THAT'S WHY IT'S CALLED THE "PRESENT."
(05.09.2024)

6. On Beauty

ONCE YOU LEARN TO SEE THE BEAUTY
IN EVERYTHING YOU CAN SEE
THE DIVINE IN EVERYTHING.

BECAUSE **BEAUTY IS**
INDISTINGUISHABLE
FROM DIVINITY.
(NOVEMBER 2022)

EXTERNAL BEAUTIFICATION GRANTS
INTERNAL GRATIFICATION.
(08.12.2022)

YOU CAN'T TELL BEAUTY FROM DIVINITY.
(14.12.2022)

I ONCE HEARD SOMEONE SAY*
SOMETHING TO THE TUNE OF "THE
PURPOSE OF LUXURY IS TO SIGNAL TO
YOUR BRAIN THAT IT'S SAFE TO TAKE
CREATIVE RISKS" AND I THINK THAT'S,
TO A LARGE DEGREE, ALSO TRUE FOR
BEAUTY.
(07.03.2023)

*THE QUOTES:
"*LUXURY IS A SIGNAL TO YOUR BRAIN
THAT YOU CAN AFFORD TO TAKE RISK.*"
"*THE GREAT MEANING OF LUXURY IS
THAT IT'S AN INPUT TO CREATIVITY.*"
— ERIC WEINSTEIN

LIFE IS FUCKING MAGIC.
STOP TELLING YOURSELF IT ISN'T.
YOU'RE JUST LYING TO YOURSELF.
(05.05.2023)

I AM DISTURBED BY THE BEAUTY. IT
KEEPS COMING BACK TO ME IN FLASHES,
VISIONS. THEY HAUNT ME. THEY ALL DO.
THEY REMIND ME OF WHAT I'VE MISSED,
REMIND ME OF MY FAILURES. BY NOT
MAKING THEM FALL HEAD-OVER-HEELS
FOR ME, MY FAILURES CONTINUE.
PERHAPS THIS IS WHY THERE'S ALWAYS
THIS LINGERING SENSE OF TRAGEDY
WHENEVER I MEET SOMEONE TRULY,
DIVINELY BEAUTIFUL.

(15.08.2023)

OF COURSE I SEEK BEAUTY IN LIFE.
I THRIVE IN IT. LIKE OXYGEN
FOR THE BRAIN, IS BEAUTY
FOR THE SOUL.

(29.09.2023)

IF HEAVEN HAD A FACE
IT WOULD LOOK LIKE YOU.

(03.05.2024)

CHIVALRY IS THE ROOT OF ROMANCE;
GRACE IS THE STALK;
COMPASSION IS THE LEAVES;
AND LOVE IS THE FLOWER
THAT BLOOMS.
AND WHAT IS THE SEED?
WELL, IT IS BEAUTY, OF COURSE.
(19.07/12.08.2024)

TAKE THE SHIT LIFE THROWS AT YOU
AND USE IT TO FERTILIZE YOUR GARDEN.
THAT'S ALCHEMY,
THAT'S THE ARTIST'S WAY,
AND IT'S ALSO
REDEMPTION.
(17.09.2024)

7. On Oneness

EVERYTHING IS RECIPROCAL,
EVERYTHING IS CONNECTED.
IT'S THE SIMPLE LAW OF KARMA.
(NOVEMBER 2022)

MOST OF THE COSMIC
INTERCONNECTEDNESS CAN NEVER BE
EXPLAINED LOGICALLY.
(21.11.2022)

EVERYTHING IS CONNECTED SO THERE
IS NO BEGINNING OR END TO
ANYTHING.
(28.11.2022)

THE POWERS OF THE UNIVERSE ARE
INFINITE AND WITH GREAT POWER
COMES GREAT RESPONSIBILITY.
(26.12.2022)

EVERYTHING IS A REFLECTION
OF EVERYTHING.
(DECEMBER 2022)

THE WHOLE UNIVERSE IS FREQUENCY,
VIBRATION. THAT MEANS IT'S ALL MUSIC.
THAT MEANS IT'S ALL DANCE.
EMBRACE IT.
(15.02.2023)

WE ARE ALL JUST DIFFERENT
EXPRESSIONS OF THE SAME UNDERLYING
ENERGY, SO WE ARE ALL ONE.
YOU ARE THE WORLD
AND THE WORLD IS YOU,
AND THERE IS NO PAST NOR FUTURE,
THERE IS ONLY NOW.
(MARCH 2023)

ON A VERY BASIC, ABSOLUTELY
FUNDAMENTAL LEVEL, EVERYTHING IS AN
EXPRESSION OF GOD, SO EVERYTHING IS
THE SAME, SO EVERYTHING IS ONE.

(MARCH 2023)

EGO IS HOW WE INTERACT WITH THE
REST OF US. SO IT IS IMPORTANT. BUT
THE KNOWLEDGE OF THE UNDERLYING
UNITY, OF THE ONENESS, MUST BE THERE
FIRST. OTHERWISE, THE EGO BECOMES
SELF-ABSORBED, AND THAT'S WHEN ALL
SORTS OF PROBLEMS BEGIN. AND
KNOWLEDGE IS NOT INFORMATION,
NOT THEORY. REAL KNOWLEDGE COMES
FROM EXPERIENCE.

(13.03.2023)

I AM THE WORLD AND THE WORLD IS
ME. IT IS NOT SOMETHING THAT I
KNOW, IT IS SOMETHING THAT I FEEL.

(13.03.2023)

SPIRITUALITY IS THE SAME AS RELIGION.
RELIGION IS JUST A HOLISTIC WAY OF
EXPERIENCING REALITY. THAT'S ALL IT IS.
THERE IS NOTHING SUPERNATURAL
TO IT.
(17.03.2023)

THE THING ABOUT GOD, IS THAT IT
ALSO WANTS TO EXPERIENCE PAIN AND
DEATH. BECAUSE OTHERWISE, IT
WOULDN'T KNOW WHAT JOY AND LIFE
ARE.
(18.03.2023)

A REAL RELIGION, OR REAL SPIRITUALITY,
IS SUPPOSED TO BE A DESCRIPTION OF
THE TRUTH. RIGHT NOW, ALL WE HAVE
ARE DESCRIPTIONS OF RULES.
(20.03.2023)

WE ARE A TREE. THERE IS THE TAO, THE TREE BARK THAT SUPPORTS AND NURTURES US. WE MAKE UP ALL THE BRANCHES AND LEAVES. IT IS OUR JOB TO MAKE SURE THE TREE DOESN'T DIE AND KEEPS GROWING BIGGER AND STRONGER.

(23.03.2023)

THE SYSTEM HAS CREATED DIVISION WITHOUT US REALIZING IT'S DIVISION. RELIGION AND MONEY ARE THE SAME. RELIGION AND SCIENCE ARE THE SAME. EDUCATION AND MORALITY ARE THE SAME. LOVE AND ETHICS ARE THE SAME. THERE IS NO DIVISION. THERE IS NO FRAGMENTATION. WE ARE ALL ONE.

(24.03.2023)

MERGE YOUR THOUGHTS, YOUR EGO AND THE VASTNESS INTO ONE. YOU NEED NO DRUGS AND NO HELP FOR THAT. IT'S JUST YOU.

(27.04.2023)

THE BASE LEVEL IS 0, NOTHINGNESS.
EVERYTHING ELSE IS EXTRA.
WHAT THAT "EVERYTHING ELSE"
EXACTLY IS, IS UP TO US TO DECIDE.
(23.05.2023)

PERHAPS THE BIGGEST TRAGEDY OF OUR
TIMES IS THAT PEOPLE ARE SO
DETACHED FROM THEIR HIGHER SELVES
THAT THEY FAIL TO SEE THE HOLINESS
WITHIN THEMSELVES AND OTHERS.
THUS, THEY FAIL TO SERVE AND
EMBRACE THAT HOLINESS, THUS FAILING
BOTH AS INDIVIDUALS ("INDIVIDUAL"
MEANS INDIVISIBLE - BUT THEY ARE
ALREADY DIVIDED) AND AS A SPECIES.
(04.08.2023)

THE CLOSER YOU GET TO YOUR TRUE
SELF, THE SOURCE, THE UNIVERSE, GOD,
WHATEVER YOU WANNA CALL IT, THE
FASTER AND MORE DIRECTLY THE
MECHANISMS OF CAUSE AND EFFECT,
ALSO KNOWN AS KARMA, WILL START
MANIFESTING. JUST PAY ATTENTION.
(23.08.2023)

I'M ALL ABOUT PERSONAL
EMPOWERMENT. AT THE SAME TIME, I'M
ALSO OF THE BELIEF THAT ONE MUST
RECOGNIZE THAT THERE IS A HIGHER
POWER ABOVE THEM, ONE THAT COULD
BE DESCRIBED AS THE COLLECTIVE
CONSCIOUSNESS, WHICH IS WHERE WE
ALL COME FROM AND WHERE WE GO.
THE INFINITE, IN WHICH THE
CONSTRAINTS OF TIME AND SPACE CEASE
TO EXIST.
(05.09.2023)

FOR EACH THING THAT UNITES US,
THERE ARE 100 THINGS THAT DIVIDE US.
WE JUST HAVE TO FOCUS
ON THE THINGS THAT UNITE US.
(11.10.2023)

IT'S NOT ABOUT WHAT YOU CAN ASK
FROM GOD.
IT'S ABOUT WHAT GOD CAN ASK
FROM YOU.
(24.10.2023)

NONE OF THIS IS ABOUT YOU.
(01.03.2024)

In order to move on, you need to not only stop feeling sorry for yourself, but also stop feeling sorry for the world. That is forgiveness in its essence. To give up a certain lens to see things for what they are, and what they could be.

(27.03.2024)

Remember the famous phrase: "Divide and conquer."

What you are witnessing, most likely, is the divide. It is an illusion. There is no division. There is no "us and them."

There is only us.

(10.08.2024)

8. On Individuation

EMBRACE WHO YOU ARE BECOMING.

(12.11.2022)

BE KIND TO YOURSELF.

BUT ALSO, BE HARD ON YOURSELF.

(19.11.2022)

ONE OF THE GOALS IN THE GAME OF
LIFE IS TO GIVE AWAY AS MUCH OF
YOURSELF AS POSSIBLE BEFORE THE
ACTUAL DEATH.

(03.12.2022)

IF YOU DON'T PUNISH YOURSELF FOR
THE THINGS YOU HAVE LEFT UNDONE
OR HAVEN'T DONE PROPERLY, THEN LIFE
WILL PUNISH YOU FOR YOU, AND LIFE
WILL BE MUCH MORE BRUTAL IN HER
CHOICE OF PUNISHMENT.

(09.01.2023)

BY JOURNALLING YOU CAN LEARN
ABOUT ALL THE THINGS YOU DIDN'T
KNOW YOU KNEW.

(12.01.2023)

I DO NOT ALLOW MYSELF TO COMPLAIN
OR BITCH OR WHINE ABOUT ANYTHING.
IT'S UNPRODUCTIVE.

(15.01.2023)

DO NOT GIVE A FUCK WHETHER YOU
COME OFF AS WEIRD OR A BIT CRAZY OR
WHATEVER. IT'S FINE. IT'S YOU. EMBRACE
YOURSELF, EMBRACE THE AWKWARDNESS.
LIKE ANYTHING, IT IS ONLY TEMPORARY.
AND YOU NEVER KNOW WHAT YOU
MIGHT FIND IF YOU OVERCOME IT.

(02.03.2023)

A CERTAIN DEGREE OF VULNERABILITY CAN BE EXTREMELY USEFUL. YOU GO FOR A WALK, BAREFOOT, YOU'RE GOING TO HAVE TO WATCH WHERE YOU STEP. SO IT HELPS YOU BECOME MORE AWARE. PHYSICAL VULNERABILITY HELPS US IDENTIFY AND MITIGATE OUTSIDE THREATS. EMOTIONAL VULNERABILITY HELPS US IDENTIFY AND MITIGATE INSIDE THREATS, THE THINGS THAT TRIGGER YOU. THE OLD SAYING "STRONG OPINIONS LOOSELY HELD" ALSO CONVEYS VULNERABILITY, INTELLECTUAL VULNERABILITY - REALLY BELIEVE IN WHAT YOU BELIEVE IN, BUT BE READY TO CHANGE YOUR PERSPECTIVE IF YOU ARE PROVEN WRONG OR WHEN CIRCUMSTANCES CHANGE.

(06.03.2023)

EVERY BATTLE YOU EVER HAVE TO FIGHT IS A BATTLE WITH YOURSELF.

(19.03.2023)

"Just be yourself."

Yeah, you should, but good luck with that. People don't REALLY want you to be yourself, they want you to be the image of you that they've constructed. In addition, do you even know what the real you looks like outside of those constructs? Outside of the constructs you yourself have created, by analyzing, by thinking how you could be and should be, by being in conflict with who you actually are? And simply by the very nature of you being brought up in a society, in a culture. It's not an easy task to view yourself without those preconceived images, whether they are positive or negative.

What if the actual you is not who you think it is?

(24.04.2023)

Maybe I have lost it. I mean, there's a probability and it would be foolish to disregard that probability. However, that is not a question just for me and just for now, that is what all of us must ask ourselves at all times: Have I lost it? Am I on the right path? Are my thoughts and actions aligned with the direction and energies I want them to be? Are the mental models and frameworks I work within consistent with what I know and sense about the nature of reality and my place in it?

Do I know my place in it?

Or have I, truly and utterly, lost it?

(16.06.2023)

YOUR LIMITATIONS ARE WHAT MAKE
YOU UNIQUE. THANKS TO YOUR
LIMITATIONS, YOU ARE ABLE TO HAVE
PERSPECTIVES THAT WOULD BE EASY TO
MISS OTHERWISE. THANKS TO YOUR
LIMITATIONS, YOU WILL BE ABLE TO
CREATE BIGGER MEANING AND PAY
MORE ATTENTION TO ANYTHING THAT'S
WITHIN THOSE LIMITATIONS. THEY HELP
YOU FOCUS.

(19.06.2023)

I AM ALIVE. TO BE ALIVE IS TO BE ABLE
TO ACT. TO BE ABLE TO ACT IS TO BE
ABLE TO CHANGE, AND TO EXPERIENCE.

(27.06.2023)

THIS IS WHO I AM. AND I NEED TO
FULLY EMBODY WHO I AM IN ORDER TO
EMBRACE WHO I AM BECOMING.

(27.06.2023)

TO LIVE, COMFORTABLY, WITH DEATH BY
YOUR SIDE, IS TO TRULY LIVE.

(27.06.2023)

THE FINAL BOSS THAT YOU HAVE TO
DEFEAT IS YOURSELF. GOOD LUCK.

(17.12.2023)

THINGS YOU WILL INEVITABLY FIND ON
THE QUEST TO FIND YOUR TRUE SELF:

1. DISCOMFORT

2. LONELINESS

3. NEW PERSPECTIVES

4. "FUCK THIS, I'M TOO TIRED"

5. FIRE

6. YOUR DEMONS

(17.12.2023)

I'M KNOWN TO BE A LOT OF THINGS.
"SANE" ISN'T ONE OF THEM.

(26.12.2023)

OWN YOUR STORY.

(04.01.2024)

I AM NOT CONCERNED WITH WHAT
OTHERS THINK OF ME. THAT'S THEIR
BUSINESS. I AM CONCERNED, HOWEVER,
WITH WHAT I THINK OF OTHERS. THAT'S
MY BUSINESS, THAT'S WHAT I CONTROL.
AND FUNNILY ENOUGH, IT TELLS ME A
LOT MORE ABOUT MYSELF THAN THE
OTHERS.

(07.07.2023/23.02.2024)

WHY WOULD YOU EVER DOUBT
YOURSELF? YOU CAN ONLY BE YOU.
YOU CAN NEVER BE ANYONE ELSE.

(27.02.2024)

TRANSCENDENCE IS REALIZING YOU
WERE THE CITADEL ALL ALONG.

(28.02.2024)

IF YOU EVER FEEL WORTHLESS, JUST REMEMBER THAT SO WAS BITCOIN FOR THE FIRST YEAR OF ITS EXISTENCE. IT'S ALSO WORTH NOTING THAT IT DIDN'T CHANGE ITSELF IN ORDER TO GO FROM 0 TO A $1T+ ASSET. ALL IT DID WAS:

1. BE ITSELF

2. NOT DIE

IF YOU DO THOSE TWO THINGS, THE WORLD WILL HAVE TO RECKON WITH YOU.

(15.03.2024)

"THE NATURE OF BITCOIN IS SUCH THAT ONCE VERSION 0.1 WAS RELEASED, THE CORE DESIGN WAS SET IN STONE FOR THE REST OF ITS LIFETIME."

— SATOSHI NAKAMOTO

IN THE CURRENT ZEITGEIST, "SELF-LOVE" IS USED AS AN EXCUSE FOR SEDATION, ESCAPISM AND IGNORANCE. IN REALITY, IT SHOULD BE AN AVENUE OF HONESTY, INTROSPECTION AND ATTENTIVENESS.

(11.04.2024)

MY ONLY COMPETITION IS MYSELF. I AM LITERALLY IN A LEAGUE OF MY OWN.

(18.04.2024)

ALL THIS TIME I WAS LOOKING FOR EXTERNAL VALIDATION TO MY IDEAS...

WHEREAS I SHOULD HAVE BEEN LOOKING FOR INTERNAL AND EXPERIENTIAL VALIDATION.

HOW SILLY OF ME.

(25.04.2024)

I THINK WE TEND TO ATTACH OUR EGOS TO OUR IDEAS TOO MUCH. WE CLAIM IDEAS (AND IDEOLOGIES) AS "OURS" AND AS SUCH, WE DEFINE OURSELVES AS THOSE IDEAS, AND WE GET OFFENDED IF SOMEONE CHALLENGES OR CRITICIZES THEM. IN REALITY, IDEAS ARE JUST "OUT THERE," LIKE A FIELD WHERE YOU CAN PICK YOURS, OR RADIO STATIONS THAT YOU CAN TUNE IN AND OUT OF, OR LIKE LOVE, OR GOD. NONE OF THOSE ARE ANYBODY'S, YET THEY'RE EVERYBODY'S. THEY ARE ALSO NOT STATIC. LIKE LIFE ITSELF, THOSE CONCEPTS AND THE MEANINGS ASSIGNED TO THOSE WORDS AND PHENOMENA EVOLVE AND CHANGE OVER TIME, ACCORDING TO THE CULTURE, ENVIRONMENT AND CIRCUMSTANCES.

(24/25.06.2024)

When you first start getting in shape, or getting into "your thing," your friends and family will cheer you on. They will (generally) compliment you, encourage you, show their support. When you get deep into your craft, they will go silent.

They will see you as obsessed, they might even become concerned about your health. That's how you'll know you're on your way to something really great.

That's how you'll know you're pushing the boundaries.

(26.06.2024)

PEOPLE DON'T WANT TO KNOW WHAT YOU REALLY THINK. THEY DON'T WANT TO HEAR ORIGINAL, UNCONVENTIONAL, PARADIGM-SHIFTING THOUGHTS. THEY WANT TO HEAR SOMEBODY ELSE SAY WHAT THEY ALREADY THINK. THIS IS WHY MOST OF SOCIAL MEDIA IS DESIGNED TO KEEP US IN OUR OWN LITTLE BUBBLES. THIS IS WHY CONFORMITY IS SUCH AN ISSUE. IN ORDER TO GROW AS A PERSON, YOU HAVE TO BURST YOUR OWN BUBBLE.

LET YOUR ONLY ASSUMPTION BE THAT YOU DON'T REALLY KNOW ANYTHING.

(25.07.2024)

I'M NOT AFRAID TO BE WRONG. I WOULD RATHER THINK ABOUT THINGS, AND COME TO THE WRONG CONCLUSIONS, THAN NOT THINK ABOUT THEM AT ALL AND JUST BLINDLY ACCEPT WHATEVER THE CURRENT CONSENSUS IS.

(05.08.2024)

IN ORDER TO GET A NEW PERSPECTIVE,
RISE UP.
(13.08.2024)

THE ONLY TIME WHEN YOU CAN
BECOME THE PERSON YOU WANT TO BE
IS RIGHT NOW.
BECAUSE THE ONLY TIME THAT REALLY
EXISTS IS THE PRESENT.
THE PAST IS AN ABSTRACTION,
THE FUTURE IS A PROJECTION.
(28.08.2024)

BECOMING THE CHANGE YOU WANT TO
SEE IN THE WORLD IS NOT EASY WHEN
THE WORLD DOES NOT WANT TO SEE
YOU CHANGE.
(03.09.2024)

You are not who you were or what you did. You are who you are and what you do now.

Approach people with an open heart and a smile and they will see you accordingly. You are the master of your fate. The harbinger of light. The provider of inspiration.

Through you, God can speak, and you can make the word of God audible.

Never be ashamed of who you are and what you're here to do.

Courage, confidence and compassion are innate parts of you that should be celebrated.

Carry yourself in accordance with that.

(23.09.2024)

WHAT STRIKES ME IS THAT AS I FIND
MYSELF LACKING IN SOME OF THE
THINGS I CONSIDER SO VERY ESSENTIAL
TO ONE'S WELL-BEING, THEN WHAT I'M
PRESENTED WITH IS, IN A VERY
PROFOUND SENSE, A SET OF
CIRCUMSTANCES THAT ARE ALMOST AS IF
DESIGNED FOR ME TO GO ON AND FIND
THAT WHICH SUPPORTS ME WHEN
NOTHING ELSE DOES. IT'S LIKE:
"YOU'RE ON YOUR OWN NOW.
DEAL WITH IT. MAKE PEACE WITH IT."
(29.09.2024)

EVEN IF THE WHOLE WORLD IS
A SIMULATION, THEN YOU ARE
THE OPERATING SYSTEM.
YOU CAN REWRITE YOUR CODE.
(15.02.2023/12.10.2024)

STOP COMPARING YOURSELF
TO PEOPLE WHO ARE NOT DOING
WHAT YOU'RE DOING.
(14.10.2024)

WHY DO YOU CARE ABOUT FITTING IN
WITH "NORMAL" PEOPLE?
ARE THEY DOING THE THINGS YOU
WANT TO DO?
ARE THEY WHERE OR WHO YOU
WANT TO BE?
NO?
THEN WHY WOULD YOU CARE?
YOU SHOULD EMBRACE THE FACT
THAT YOU'RE NOT FITTING IN.
STARS DON'T FIT IN BOXES,
ONLY SQUARES FIT IN BOXES.
(24.10.2024)

9. On Motivation & Perseverance

Do what you dare.

No one will care.

(12.11.2022)

It's not a day off. There's never a day off when you are on a mission and realizing your full potential. The work is constant, as is play.

(26.11.2022)

Yesterday, I was a loser.

Today, I am a winner.

(02.01.2023)

Everything is a projection of power.

(11.01.2023)

I don't need a reward
for doing all this.
Doing all this
is the reward.
(21.01.2023)

Raise the standards.
Strive for exceptional excellence.
Raise the consciousness.
(23.01.2023)

It's okay to fail.
It's not okay to not try.
(26.01.2023)

Dare to look on the other side.
(04.02.2023)

I FUCKING LOVE PROBLEMS. I LOVE
FEELING DOWN, SAD AND DEPRESSED.
AND ALONE. AND UNLOVED. BECAUSE
THEN I HAVE SOMETHING TO DO, TO
FIX, TO CREATE. I ESPECIALLY LOVE
HAVING NOTHING AT ALL. BECAUSE
THEN I HAVE NOTHING TO LOSE. THERE
ARE NO ATTACK VECTORS AGAINST ME.

(04.02.2023)

YOU'RE ALWAYS TIRED. GET OVER IT.
WORK AROUND IT.

(09.02.2023)

LEARN IN PUBLIC. MAKE ART IN PUBLIC.
WORK OUT IN PUBLIC. FAIL IN PUBLIC.
AND SUCCEED IN PUBLIC. THAT'S THE
BEST WAY TO INSPIRE OTHERS AND ALSO
THE BEST WAY TO HOLD YOURSELF
ACCOUNTABLE FOR WHAT THE FUCK
YOU'RE DOING.

(15.02.2023)

"I'M TOO OLD FOR THIS,"

SAYS THE 30-YEAR OLD. IT'S LIKE, BRO.
THE VERY FACT THAT YOU ARE SAYING
THIS SHOWS HOW MUCH OF A FUCKING
CHILD YOU STILL ARE. DON'T DISCOUNT
YOURSELF. YOU ARE CAPABLE OF SO
MUCH MORE THAN YOU THINK YOU ARE.
(04.03.2023)

IF SOMETHING BOTHERS YOU, THEN IT
IS YOU THAT HAS TO DO SOMETHING
ABOUT IT. NOT ANYBODY ELSE. BECAUSE
IT BOTHERS YOU. IT IS SPEAKING TO
YOU.
(07.03.2023)

THERE MUST BE NO FEAR.
THERE MUST ONLY BE TRUTH.
(12.03.2023)

PROBLEMS ARE YOUR BIGGEST
STRENGTH. THEY ARE WEALTH IN THE
FORM OF THE POTENTIAL VALUE YOU
CAN CREATE BY SOLVING THEM. EVEN IF
YOU DON'T SOLVE THEM (ALL), YOU STILL
GET EXPERIENCE, WHICH IS
KNOWLEDGE, WHICH IS INVALUABLE.
THE BIGGER THE PROBLEM, THE
GREATER THE OPPORTUNITY.

(15.03.2023)

I DON'T BELIEVE IN TALENT, AND I
DON'T BELIEVE IN THEORY. I DO BELIEVE
IN PRACTICE AND EXPERIENCE. TALENT
AND THEORY ARE THE RESULTS, THE
EXPRESSIONS OF PRACTICE AND
EXPERIENCE, AND NOT THE
PRECONDITIONS OR THE MEANS.

(17.03.2023)

WE CAN STILL FIGURE ALL THIS OUT
BEFORE AI DOES.

(03.04.2023)

TWO EASY STEPS TO GET
SMARTER/LEARN A NEW SKILL FAST:

1. ASSUME/RECOGNIZE THAT YOU ARE
DUMB AND KNOW NOTHING

2. ASSUME THAT ALL YOUR TEACHERS
ARE EVEN DUMBER AND KNOW EVEN
LESS

(03.04.2023)

WHAT DO YOU MEAN I HAVE NOTHING?
MATE. I HAVE AN IDEA. I HAVE A VISION.
THAT'S MORE THAN MOST PEOPLE WILL
EVER HAVE.

(21.04.2023)

IF I DON'T BELIEVE IN WHAT I DO,
THEN WHO WILL?

(01.05.2023)

I REFUSE TO WORK ON THINGS
I DON'T CARE ABOUT.
(05.05.2023)

YOUR GOVERNMENT IS NOT GOING TO
HELP YOU. YOUR FRIENDS ARE NOT
GOING TO HELP YOU. YOUR FAMILY IS
NOT GOING TO HELP YOU. YOUR
HEROES, SAINTS OR DEITIES ARE NOT
GOING TO HELP YOU. YOU HAVE TO
HELP YOU.
(13.05.2023)

I HAVE DECIDED THAT I WILL NOT
BE BOTHERED BY THE BULLSHIT.
I WILL FOCUS ON THE SIGNAL.
(14.05.2023)

ONE DAY YOU WILL LOOK BACK AT THIS
TIME AND IT WILL ALL MAKE SENSE.
(20.05.2023)

"WHAT IF I WILL NEVER BE ENOUGH?"
WELL, THAT'S A POSSIBILITY. BUT AS
LONG AS YOU'RE HERE, YOU CAN GIVE IT
YOUR BEST SHOT. AND AS YOU KNOW,
YOU MISS 100% OF THE SHOTS YOU
DON'T TAKE. SO AIM. TAKE THE SHOT.
YOU MAY MISS, BUT YOU CAN SHOOT
AGAIN.

(21.05.2023)

INTERESTING. INTENSE. INSPIRING.
INCREDIBLY LONELY.

(24.05.2023)

TRY. FAIL. GO TO SLEEP. TRY AGAIN. FAIL.
GO TO SLEEP. TRY AGAIN. FAIL. GO TO
SLEEP. TRY AGAIN. WIN. GO TO SLEEP.
TRY AGAIN.

(30.05.2023)

STEP #1: PROOF OF WORK.

NOW HERE'S THE KICKER.

THERE IS NO STEP #2.

IT'S. ALWAYS. WORK.

BUT THIS SIMPLY MEANS THAT YOU
HAVE TO EMBODY YOUR HIGHER SELF
THROUGH YOUR WORK,
THROUGH YOUR WHOLE BEING.

AND THINK OF HOW THE TERM
"PROOF OF WORK" CAN ALSO MEAN:
VERIFIABLE DATA THAT PROVES
THAT AN IDEA WORKS.

(13.06.2023)

ZOOM OUT.

LOWER YOUR TIME PREFERENCE.

DON'T CHASE THE EASY, FREQUENT, MEANINGLESS DOPAMINE HITS.

CHASE THE HARD, INFREQUENT, MEANINGFUL DOPAMINE HITS.

THERE'S A LOT OF SUFFERING ON THAT PATH, YES.

BUT IF YOU ZOOM OUT ENOUGH, AND AT THE SAME TIME, ARE PRESENT ENOUGH, THEN YOU WILL BE ABLE TO TIE THAT DOPAMINE RELEASE TO THE PROCESS OF WORKING TOWARDS THAT GOAL ITSELF, INSTEAD OF THE RESULT OF "REACHING" THE GOAL.

AND ONCE YOU ENJOY THAT, ONCE YOU ARE ABLE TO FIND PLEASURE IN SUFFERING, THEN NOTHING SHORT OF DEATH CAN STAND BETWEEN YOU, YOUR HIGHEST POTENTIAL, AND YOUR DESTINY.

(19.06.2023)

FOR THE LONGEST TIME, MY
OVERARCHING MODE OF BEING WAS:
"I'LL SEE WHAT HAPPENS."
NOW IT'S LIKE:
"I SEE WHAT HAPPENS.
I'LL HELP US GET THERE."
(30.07.2023)

DISCIPLINE SUPERSEDES TALENT.
(30.07.2023)

BUILD YOUR OWN FUTURE.
MAKE YOUR OWN REALITY.
DEFY THE RULES OF GRAVITY.
FIGHT THE FOUL DEPRAVITY.
(03.08.2023)

THE BEST SWORDS ARE FORGED
IN A SCORCHING HEAT.
(14.08.2023)

YOU DON'T BECOME "THE BEST VERSION
OF YOURSELF" BY IGNORING THE WORST
VERSION OF YOURSELF. YOU JUST DON'T.
YOU BECOME THE BEST VERSION OF
YOURSELF BY WORKING WITH THE
WORST VERSION OF YOURSELF.
(28.08.2023)

WINNERS ARE LOSERS
WHO DON'T GIVE UP.
&
WINNERS ARE LOVERS
WHO DON'T GIVE UP.
(03.09.2023)

WINNERS DO GIVE UP. CONSTANTLY
AND WITHOUT REGRETS. THEY GIVE UP
THINGS LIKE: TOXIC RELATIONSHIPS,
MEANINGLESS JOBS, THE URGE TO
CONFORM, PARTYING, IDEAS THAT
DON'T SERVE THEM, BAD HABITS - EVEN
IF THOSE BAD HABITS ARE SO
INGRAINED INTO THE CULTURE THAT
THEY ARE CALLED "TRADITION." IN FACT,
THEY GIVE UP THEIR WHOLE LIVES,
EVERY NIGHT, IN ORDER TO LIVE NEW
AND BETTER ONES TOMORROW.

(08/19.09.2023)

YOU ARE THE FOREFATHER OF YOUR
DYNASTY. ACT ACCORDINGLY.

(19.09.2023)

GOOD THINGS WILL NOT HAPPEN
UNLESS YOU MAKE THEM HAPPEN.

(03.10.2023)

As soon as I start thinking of it as "work" I start avoiding it. So that is a division, a dichotomy I still have to get over. The distinction between work and play. They're one and the same.
(07.10.2023)

Look.
Things are only difficult if you think they're difficult.
(07.10.2023)

Be a nobody on the way to becoming somebody.
(08.10.2023)

By being passionate, is how you get the people you need to work with, to work with you.
(11.10.2023)

YOU NEED TO LEARN TO THINK BIGGER.
GO WHEREVER YOU NEED TO, DO
WHATEVER YOU NEED TO - TO MAKE
YOURSELF AND YOUR BUSINESS
SUCCESSFUL.

(18.10.2023)

TO REALLY ADVANCE IN PHYSICAL AND
MENTAL EXERCISE, YOU HAVE TO BE
PUSHING YOURSELF TO (AND OVER) THE
LIMITS. LIFE TENDS TO DO THE SAME. IT
WILL PRESENT YOU WITH GREATER AND
GREATER CHALLENGES FOR YOU TO
EVOLVE. DON'T GET SCARED NOW.

(20.10.2023)

A GOOD GAME GENERALLY GETS
MORE DIFFICULT AS YOU PROGRESS
THROUGH THE LEVELS.
WHY WOULD YOU EXPECT LIFE
TO BE ANY DIFFERENT?

(08.11.2023)

YOU ARE A NOBODY? GOOD. YOU HAVE
NOTHING? EVEN BETTER.

A PRINCE BECOMING A KING IS BORING,
IT'S JUST THE WAY OF LIFE.

A PEASANT BECOMING A KING,
HOWEVER...

(08.11.2023)

I WILL NOT RELY UPON ANYONE OR
ANYTHING. I WILL BE THE ONE RELIED
UPON.

(26.11.2023)

YOU JUST HAVE TO BELIEVE. THERE IS NO
OTHER WAY. FRUSTRATION IS A WASTE.
DISAPPOINTMENT IS A PROJECTION.

(09.12.2023)

WEAK PEOPLE MAKE EXCUSES AS TO WHY
THEY CAN'T BE STRONG.

STRONG PEOPLE MAKE EXCUSES AS TO
WHY THEY CAN'T BE WEAK.

(16.12.2023)

You wouldn't be presented with challenges and hardship unless you were ready to face them.

So face them.

All of this, and I mean all of it, only exists with the sole purpose of providing us the ability to learn and grow as souls in order for us to "return home" as we find our true selves.

If we shy away from the trials and tribulations presented to us, we shy away from those paths of learning as well as the path to our highest selves, leaving us stuck in a loop of the same experiences, same mistakes, same restlessness (Samskara).

(02.01.2024)

SHIT IS SUPPOSED TO BREAK YOU
DOWN SO YOU COULD BUILD
YOURSELF UP. THAT'S THE BLESSING
AND THE CURSE.

(02.01.2024)

IF YOU DO NOT FAIL,
THEN YOU ARE NOT SETTING
YOUR GOALS HIGH ENOUGH.

(02.01.1024)

YOU HAVE TO FORGO SOMETHING.
SACRIFICE. OPEN THE DARKEST CLOSETS
FIRST. EAT THE FROGS. EVERY DAY.

DO THE SHIT YOU DON'T WANT TO DO,
BUT KNOW IS GOOD FOR YOU.

THAT'S THE 20% THAT'S GOING TO GET
YOU 80% OF THE WAY.

(03.01.2024)

THE RESTLESSNESS...

IT EXISTS FOR A REASON.

PUT IT TO USE.

(04.01.2024)

WITH EVERYTHING AND ANYTHING, IT
COMES DOWN TO 2 FUNDAMENTAL
QUESTIONS:

1. WHY DO YOU WANT IT?

2. HOW BAD DO YOU WANT IT?

(04.01.2024)

IF YOU WANT EVERYTHING

YOU HAVE TO BE READY

TO SACRIFICE EVERYTHING.

(04.01.2024)

Do it or discard it. Don't "to-do" it and don't dwell on it, whenever possible. Otherwise, it's extra weight on your shoulders, extra thoughts in your head.
That's the stuff that doesn't let you sleep at night, or doesn't let you focus on your life's task.
Clear the to-do list, clear your mind, and in doing so, you clear your path and free your spirit.
(05.01.2024)

Live for the moments when you feel like you could die because you have given everything, but also, can't...
For the same reason.
(06.01.2024)

LIFE SAYS SHE'S GOING TO INFLICT
EVEN MORE PAIN?
I SAY BRING IT ON, BITCH.
FUCKING TRY.
PULL ME DOWN, I'LL SHOOT BACK UP.
FOR THE OPPOSITE TO HAPPEN
YOU'LL HAVE TO END ME.
(16.02.2024)

YOU'RE STILL A LOSER.
TRY AGAIN, TRY HARDER.
(25.02.2024)

WHENEVER YOU SWITCH YOUR CORE
MODE OF BEING FROM "CHASE" TO
"ATTRACT," THERE ARE 2 THINGS:

1. RESISTANCE

2. LAG

RESISTANCE MEANS YOU ACTUALLY HAVE
TO WORK ON YOURSELF, WANT TO
CHANGE, AND BE READY FOR THAT
CHANGE. LAG SIMPLY MEANS IT TAKES
TIME. IT COULD TAKE WEEKS. COULD
TAKE YEARS. DEPENDS ON HOW BIG IS
THE DELTA BETWEEN THE "CHASE MODE"
YOU VS THE "ATTRACT MODE" YOU.

(26.02.2024)

THE MAIN THING IS
NOT TO DOUBT YOURSELF.
KEEP TO YOUR MISSION, YOUR VIRTUES
AND YOUR HONESTY,
AND YOU SHALL SUCCEED.

(02.03.2024)

EXERCISE IS EXORCISM.
(09.03.2024)

LIFE IS NOT SUPPOSED TO GET EASIER.
IN FACT, IT'S SUPPOSED TO GET HARDER
THE BETTER YOU GET AT IT.
IT'S THE DIFFICULTY ADJUSTMENT.
(11.03.2024)

EVERY DAY, I'M HAUNTED BY THE
SHADOW OF THE MAN I COULD BE.
HE REMINDS ME TO NEVER LET
CIRCUMSTANCE DICTATE THE OUTCOME.
HE REMINDS ME TO NEVER GIVE UP.
(16.03.2024)

1. CHOOSE WHAT YOU DO, WISELY
2. DO YOUR ABSOLUTE BEST TO EXCEL
AT IT
(09.04.2024)

ALL YOU CAN REALLY DO IS
SET AN EXAMPLE.
(11.04.2024)

LIFE IS NOT GOING TO GIVE YOU
A CHANCE.
YOU'RE GOING TO HAVE TO TAKE
A CHANCE.
(12.04.2024)

REMEMBER WHO YOU ARE.
LOOK IN THE MIRROR.
YOU'RE A BEAST.
(13.04.2024)

THE PROBLEM IS NOT YOU GOING
TOO FAR.
THE PROBLEM IS YOU NOT GOING
FAR ENOUGH.
(24.04.2024)

ONE OF THE BIGGEST MISTAKES YOU
CAN MAKE IS TO ASSUME AS IF ANYONE
CARES. THEY DON'T. THEY HAVE THEIR
OWN PROBLEMS, AND THEIR OWN
DISTRACTIONS. SO YOU DO YOU. YOU
DO WHAT YOU DARE. THAT COURAGE IS
WHAT ULTIMATELY SETS YOU APART,
AND, AT SOME POINT, MAY BECOME A
FLAME OF INSPIRATION IN THE EYES OF
OTHERS.

(26.04.2024)

DON'T HOPE FOR GOOD LUCK.

WORK FOR GOOD LUCK.

(13.05.2024)

NO REST FOR THE BLESSED.

(20.05.2024)

DIVINELY INSPIRED,

BUT

DEFINITELY TIRED.

(08.06.2024)

IF YOU KNOW THAT YOUR VERY
ESSENCE - YOUR SOUL - IS CAPABLE
OF WITHSTANDING ANYTHING,
EVEN DEATH,
HOW CAN YOU BE AFRAID OF
ANYTHING?
(30.06.2024)

LUCK COMES TO THOSE
WHO WORK FOR IT.
(18.07.2024)

WE ARE LIVING IN THE BEST TIMELINE
THERE IS.
IF YOU THINK OTHERWISE YOU ARE
MERELY VICTIMIZING YOURSELF.
(31.07.2024)

YOU DON'T CONTROL THE OUTPUT.

YOU ONLY CONTROL THE INPUT.

JUST DO YOUR BEST.

AND, PERHAPS, PRAY THAT IT'S ENOUGH.

(05.08.2024)

YOU CAN BE SO MUCH,

YET YOU CHOOSE TO BE SO LITTLE.

(10.08.2024)

THE "NO" IS FREE,

THE "YES" IS EXPENSIVE.

(20.08.2024)

REMEMBER: YOU ARE NOT DOING THIS
FOR YOU, YOU ARE NOT DOING THIS
FOR THE MONEY.

YOU ARE DOING THIS FOR YOUR
FUTURE WIFE AND CHILDREN.

YOU ARE DOING THIS BECAUSE THE
WORLD NEEDS IT.

(09.09.2024)

A TEMPLE DOESN'T BUILD ITSELF.

REVERENCE.

DEVOTION.

REDEMPTION.

(12.09.2024)

ALLOW YOURSELF TO FEEL THE VICTORY
OF EVERY SMALL BATTLE
AS IF YOU HAD WON THE WAR.

(18.09.2024)

YOU HAVE TO WORK VERY HARD
TO MAKE IT LOOK REALLY EASY.

(07.10.2024)

YOU BEING ALIVE MEANS YOU ARE ONE
OF THE ACTIVE CO-CREATORS OF THIS
REALITY, WHICH MEANS YOU CAN
LITERALLY MAKE HISTORY.

(09.10.2024)

GET EXCITED FOR HAVING THE CHANCE
TO DO WHAT YOU'RE DOING. IT'S NOT A
GIVEN. THERE ARE MANY THINGS YOU
ONLY HAVE ONE SHOT AT AND YOU CAN
NEVER BE SURE WHAT AND WHEN THAT
IS. SO APPROACH EVERYTHING AS IF YOU
ONLY HAD THIS ONE CHANCE TO MAKE
IT RIGHT. ONLY ONE CHANCE TO GIVE
YOUR BEST, TO SHINE THE BRIGHTEST
YOU CAN.

(14.10.2024)

IT IS NOT ABOUT THE HOURS
YOU PUT IN.
IT'S ABOUT THE RESULT
THAT COMES OUT.

(15.10.2024)

IT'S NOT PROOF OF IDEA

IT'S NOT PROOF OF INTENTION

IT'S NOT PROOF OF VISION

IT'S NOT PROOF OF BENEVOLENCE

IT'S NOT PROOF OF CONCEPT

IT'S NOT PROOF OF INTELLIGENCE

IT'S NOT PROOF OF EXPERIENCE

IT'S NOT PROOF OF REPUTATION

IT'S NOT PROOF OF CREDENTIALS

IT'S NOT PROOF OF IMAGINATION

IT'S PROOF OF WORK.

(18.10.2024)

YOU GOTTA GET THE BASICS RIGHT
BEFORE YOU CAN TRULY MOVE FORWARD
AND ACTUALIZE YOUR HIGHEST
POTENTIAL.
KEEP AT IT.
NEVER RELENT.
DO NOT BE CONTENT WITH
MEDIOCRITY.
YOU HAVE SO MUCH TO OFFER TO THE
WORLD AND LETTING YOURSELF BECOME
THE HINDRANCE OF THAT WOULD BE
THE GREATEST SIN.
(21.10.2024)

IF YOU HAVE SHIT TO DO, JUST DO IT.
STRESSING OVER IT ONLY MAKES IT
WORSE. DOUBTING MAKES IT WORSE.
COMPLAINING MAKES IT WORSE.
(21.10.2024)

THE REAL AND ONLY QUESTION IS:
HOW BAD DO YOU WANT IT?
AND:
DO YOU **REALLY** WANT IT, DO YOU
REALLY WANT TO **DO IT** OR DO YOU JUST
WANT TO **THINK** ABOUT DOING IT?
(22.10.2024)

NONE OF US ARE BORN
FOR GREATNESS;
WE HAVE TO BE FORGED
FOR GREATNESS.
(22.10.2024)

I MAY WIN, I MAY LOSE; IT'S ALL FINE.
AT LEAST I CAN'T SAY I NEVER TRIED.
(22.10.2024)

DOING THE THINGS YOU DON'T WANT
TO DO INCREASES YOUR WILLPOWER - IN
PRIORITIZATION I SHOULD REALLY TAKE
THAT INTO ACCOUNT.

DOING THE THINGS I DON'T WANT TO
DO FIRST BOTH INCREASES MY
CONFIDENCE AS WELL AS MAKES EACH
SUBSEQUENT TASK EASIER.

(23.10.2024)

WHATEVER HAPPENS, I'LL DEAL WITH IT.

WHATEVER HAPPENS, I'LL FIGURE OUT
A WAY FORWARD.

WHATEVER HAPPENS, I'LL PROBABLY
SURVIVE.

(26.10.2024)

Work like a man.

Study like a scholar.

Exercise like an athlete.

Act like a gentleman.

Write like a poet.

(31.10.2024)

Say it loud.

Say it clear.

Say it with conviction.

(07.11.2024)

You're going to have to just do. Do more than you currently think you're capable of. But you are. And you know it. You have so much love, energy and discipline inside of you that you can't even begin to imagine. So go ahead. Push the limits. See how far you get.

(10.11.2024)

I'M BUILDING RESILIENCE.

FINDING AND MAINTAINING
EQUANIMITY AND CLARITY IN
UNCERTAINTY, IN CHAOS.

BEING ABLE TO STAND EITHER WITH OR
AGAINST FORCES OF NATURE AND NOT
LOSING YOURSELF IN THE PROCESS.
FORCES OF NATURE ARE NOT ONLY
ENVIRONMENTAL FORCES THAT HAPPEN
OUTSIDE OF US. BIOLOGY, PHYSICS,
NEUROSCIENCE - THEY ARE ALL FORCES
OF NATURE, THE HUMAN ANIMAL ITSELF
IS, AT THE CORE OF IT, AN ANIMAL JUST
LIKE ANY OTHER. HENCE, POPULAR
OPINION IS A FORCE OF NATURE. MASS
PSYCHOSIS IS A FORCE OF NATURE.
CONFORMITY, JUDGMENT, DISGUST,
LUST AND LOVE - THEY, TOO, ARE
FORCES OF NATURE. AND ONE OF THE
BEST WAYS TO PROTECT YOURSELF AND
THOSE AROUND YOU FROM SOME OF
THOSE FORCES OF NATURE IS
RESILIENCE. RELENTLESS RESILIENCE.

(12.11.2024)

You win by playing the long game.
Because the game never stops.
It's never finished.
(26.11.2024)

10. On Fate & Faith

THE SUN IS BEHIND THE CLOUD.
AND WE DON'T KNOW FOR HOW LONG.
BUT IT IS THERE, STILL THERE,
EVEN THOUGH IT'S BEHIND THE CLOUD.
(01.01.2023)

YOU CAN PLOT. YOU CAN PLAN.
BUT YOU CAN'T FIGHT THE TAO.
THE LOGOS. THE UNIVERSE.
(11.01.2023)

YOUR WHOLE LIFE IS SACRED.
YOUR WHOLE LIFE IS A RITUAL.
(10.02.2023)

I COULD ALWAYS BE WRONG.
ABOUT ANYTHING AND EVERYTHING.
IT'S JUST THAT USUALLY, I'M NOT.
(07.02/01.03.2023)

IF THE INFORMATION YOU HAVE IS
TRULY VALUABLE FOR THE WORLD, THEN
YOU DO NOT SELL IT. YOU GIVE IT AWAY
FOR FREE. LET IT DO THE GOOD THAT IT
CAN IN THE WORLD, AND KNOW THAT
BOTH YOURSELF AND OTHERS WILL BE
REWARDED FOR IT.
(09.03.2023)

LIFE IS GIVING YOU SIGNS, ALL THE
TIME. IT IS YOUR JOB TO NOTICE THEM
AND ACT ACCORDINGLY.
(09.03.2023)

IN THE ABSENCE OF THE VASTNESS WE
HAVE THE NOTHINGNESS, AND THAT IS
THE PROBLEM WE HAVE TODAY.
(14.03.2023)

I HAVE EVERYTHING I NEED.

ALL THAT'S LEFT TO DO IS BELIEVE.

(13.12.2023)

WHEN NOBODY BELIEVES IN YOU,

IT IS SIMULTANEOUSLY THE HARDEST

AND THE MOST IMPORTANT THING

TO BELIEVE IN YOURSELF.

(06.05.2024)

I AM NOT RELIGIOUS,

BUT I AM FAITHFUL.

(06.06.2024)

WHATEVER YOU NEED,

GOD WILL PROVIDE.

(02.10.2024)

11. On Lifestyle & Meaning

To be spiritual
you have to be physical.
(24.12.2022)

We are entering an age where
you can't be weak.
Or it will crush your soul.
(01.01.2023)

The first thing after waking up
or the last thing before going to
sleep SHOULD NOT be social media.
It will plant other people's
thoughts in your mind,
and you might lose track of yours.
(08.02.2023)

YOGA. EVERY. DAY.

AT FIRST, IT'S DIFFICULT TO DO.

THEN, IT WILL BE DIFFICULT

NOT TO DO.

(08.02.2023)

DANCE. LAUGHING IS DANCING.

YOGA IS DANCING.

SEX IS DANCING.

(12.02.2023)

BE WARY OF YOUR HEROES.

ANY HUMAN BEING IS FALLIBLE.

AND ANY HUMAN BEING WHO CLAIMS

TO BE ANYTHING MORE

THAN A HUMAN BEING

IS A FRAUD.

(21.02.2023)

You have too many "needs"
and too many desires.
They will sidetrack you from your
path unless you remove them.
(22.02.2023)

Your credentials are worthless
in a fake world.
(04.03.2023)

You cannot save
people who don't want to be saved.
You cannot go forward with
people who want to stand still.
(04.03.2023)

WHAT YOUR YOGA TEACHER DOESN'T
TELL YOU:

THE BEST NATURAL SUPPLEMENTS FOR
MEDITATION:

PSILOCYBIN (SPIRITUAL ENERGY)

CANNABIS (MENTAL ENERGY)

TOBACCO (PHYSICAL ENERGY)

FOR BEST RESULTS, USE
SIMULTANEOUSLY.

MY CURRENT UNDERSTANDING OF
DIFFERENT METHODS TO REACH
DIFFERENT TYPES OF MEDITATION:

ASANAS - FOR CONTACT WITH THE
EARTH, YOUR OWN PHYSICAL BODY,
AWARENESS

SITTING POSTURES - FOR CONTACT
WITH THE MENTAL LAYER

SHAVASANA - FOR CONTACT WITH THE
SPIRITUAL LAYER

FURTHER ENHANCEMENTS CAN BE MADE
BY UTILIZING MORE ENERGIES SUCH AS:

- SIGHTS (ENVIRONMENT, LIGHTING, TIME OF DAY)
- SOUNDS (MUSIC, NATURE)
- SMELLS (INCENSE, NATURE)
- PEOPLE
- LIVE FIRE

ENJOY!

(13/22.03.2023)

YOUR ALCOHOL HABITS ARE MERELY
HABITS + CONDITIONING.
YOU CAN EASILY LET GO OF BOTH.
(13.03.2023)

ACCEPTING SOMETHING WITHOUT
QUESTIONING IT IS UNACCEPTABLE.
(19.03.2023)

Jiddu Krishnamurti thinks pleasure is the source of pain.

I don't agree. It can be, but only for a sick man in a sick society. Pleasure and pain are separate ends of the same stick, and that stick is the karmic stick of consequences. In a harmonious world, pleasure is the outcome of a good decision, or value added.

A job well done, a happy wife, a healthy child, a good business.

These are the things that should bring pleasure.

Pain, on the other hand, is the outcome of a bad decision, or value destroyed.

A shoddy job, an unhappy wife, an unhealthy child, a bad business.

These are the things that should cause pain.

(19.03.2023)

A GOOD TEACHER NEVER STOPS BEING A STUDENT.

A GOOD STUDENT IS ALSO A TEACHER.

(19.03.2023)

PEOPLE LEARN EITHER THROUGH CURIOSITY OR THROUGH PAIN. HOWEVER, MOST PEOPLE ARE ALSO UNABLE TO LEARN. LEARNING DOES NOT INVOLVE REPETITION, MEMORIZING THINGS, FOLLOWING A SET OF RULES OR BEING ABLE TO WRITE A FANTASTICAL ESSAY ABOUT IT - THOSE ARE ALL THE RESULTS OF LEARNING. LEARNING IS FINDING THE SIGNAL IN THE NOISE. PAYING ATTENTION, AND MOST IMPORTANTLY, QUESTIONING.

"WHY?" IS SUCH AN IMPORTANT QUESTION.

(19.03.2023)

MOST PEOPLE DON'T WANT TO LEARN
OR ASK QUESTIONS. THEY JUST WANT
THE TRUTH. THE ANALOGY WOULD BE
THAT THEY DON'T WANT TO SOW,
MAINTAIN, OR TAKE CARE OF THE
GARDEN. NOR DO THEY WANT TO
HARVEST, NOR DO THEY WANT TO
SPEND TIME COOKING SAID HARVEST.
THEY JUST WANT TO BE SPOONFED. AND
IF YOU'RE BEING SPOONFED, THEN YOU
DON'T KNOW THE ORIGIN OF WHAT'S
BEING FED TO YOU AND IF YOU DON'T
KNOW THE ORIGIN, THEN YOU DON'T
KNOW *WHAT IT IS.*

(20.03.2023)

THE 2 GOLDEN RULES TO BUSINESS
AND RELATIONSHIPS (INCLUDING
THE RELATIONSHIP WITH YOURSELF):
UNDERPROMISE AND **OVERDELIVER**

(24.03.2023)

"WHY?" IS THE MOST IMPORTANT QUESTION WE HAVE TO ASK OURSELVES. ASK IT CONSTANTLY, AND AS MANY TIMES OVER AS YOU CAN TO GET TO THE ROOT CAUSE. ONCE YOU'RE THERE...

WHAT IS IT? IS IT ONE OF YOUR CORE VALUES AND GOALS? IF NOT, PERHAPS YOU SHOULD RE-EVALUATE YOUR ACTIONS?

(01.04.2023)

WHY ARE YOU STRESSING?

YOU HAVE LOTS TO DO, YES.

BUT THIS ONLY MEANS YOU HAVE LOTS OF ACTIVITIES TO CHOOSE FROM :)

(02.04.2023)

TOUCH GRASS.

SMOKE GRASS.

EAT GRASS-FED BEEF.

(24.06.2023)

TODAY IS A PERFECT DAY TO:

1. MEDICATE

2. MEDITATE

3. LEVITATE

SIGN OUT, TURN OFF, TUNE IN.

(25.06.2023)

I RARELY THINK.

MOSTLY, I JUST FEEL.

(07.08.2023)

MY FITNESS GOAL IS SIMPLE:

I INTEND TO BE IN BETTER PHYSICAL

SHAPE AT 50 THAN I WAS AT 30.

(14.08.2023)

MOST MEN LIKE TO GET DRUNK BECAUSE MOST MEN ARE COWARDS. ALCOHOL HELPS THEM HIDE/FORGET THE FACT. OF COURSE, IT LEADS TO THOSE MEN GETTING WEAKER AND THUS FURTHER INCREASING THE COWARDICE.

A VICIOUS CYCLE.

(21.08.2023)

WHICH DAILY ACTIONS, THOUGHTS AND WORDS BRING ME CLOSER TO MY HIGHEST GOALS?

(05.10.2023)

HOW TO BECOME MORE DECISIVE:

1. FIRST CHOICE IS USUALLY THE RIGHT CHOICE

(17.10.2023)

"YOGA EVERY DAY."

IT'S NOT A CHALLENGE, A COMPETITION, A TASK, A HABIT, A RESPONSIBILITY, A CHORE, BLACK MAGIC, VOODOO OR NEW AGE MUMBO JUMBO.

PERHAPS COUNTERINTUITIVELY, IT IS ALSO NOT DISCIPLINE, WILLPOWER OR PERSISTENCE.

AT FIRST, IT'S WORK DISGUISED AS PLAY.

THEN, IT JUST IS.

(26.10.2023)

I DON'T WANT TO "JUST GET A JOB" FOR THE SAME REASON I DON'T WANT TO "JUST GET A GIRLFRIEND" -

I WANT IT TO MEAN SOMETHING.

(17.11.2023)

Don't care about what it looks like; care about what it feels like. That is true for yoga, for dancing, for life.

(25.01.2024)

I reckon it's a good idea to alter your mantras/prayers a little bit from time to time. Just the wording or sentence structure, not necessarily the underlying intention. Why? Because if you write or say it the exact same way every time, it becomes automatic, a mechanical habit, meaning that you don't think about it anymore, which is equivalent to not even saying it. Slight changes force you to think, to stay present, and really take in the meaning behind your mantra.

(12.02.2024)

It's as much about what
you leave out
as much as it is about what
you put in.
That goes both for the mind
and the body.
(07.04.2024)

Sometimes you just need to take
things as slow as possible, for no
other reason than to cherish
them for what they are.
(26.04.2024)

I don't think you can properly
"teach" anybody other than
yourself. For others, you may act as
a guide, or an inspiration, at best.
The responsibility to learn lies
upon the learner.
(03.05.2024)

THE TO-DO LIST:

FOLLOW YOUR OBSESSIONS.

FACE YOUR PROBLEMS.

EMBRACE THE UNCERTAINTY.

PRACTICE GRATITUDE.

(03.05.2024)

TRUE CONFIDENCE IS NEVER LOUD.

IT'S ONLY THE INSECURE WHO ARE.

(15.05.2024)

YOU DON'T HATE YOUR WORK.

YOU ONLY HATE THE MEANINGLESSNESS

OF IT.

(20.05.2024)

FIND WHAT FULFILLS YOUR SPIRIT'S

DESIRES, NOT YOUR BODY'S.

(20.05.2024)

PHILOSOPHY IS - *PHÍLOS SOPHÍA* -
THE LOVE OF KNOWLEDGE, YES.
THE PURSUIT OF TRUTH, FOR SURE.
THAT ALL RESONATES WITH ME, IT HAS
MY NAME WRITTEN ALL OVER IT.
BUT WHAT REALLY CAUGHT MY
ATTENTION WAS HOW - IN MY EYES – IT
ALSO EQUATES TO A "WAY OF LIFE."
YOUR PHILOSOPHY IS HOW YOU RELATE
TO THE WORLD, WHAT IS VALUABLE FOR
YOU, WHAT IS ETHICAL FOR YOU, WHAT
"GOOD" MEANS IN YOUR PERCEPTION.
SO EVERYBODY HAS "A PHILOSOPHY,"
EVEN IF THEY DON'T ACKNOWLEDGE IT
OR PERHAPS DON'T HAVE A
PARTICULARLY INTIMATE RELATIONSHIP
WITH THE AFOREMENTIONED SOPHIA.

I THINK IT ALL RELATES A LOT TO
HAVING A PURPOSE. AND SIMILARLY TO
WHEN YOU DON'T HAVE A PURPOSE OF
YOUR OWN, YOU WILL INEVITABLY END
UP WORKING TOWARDS SOMEONE
ELSE'S; IF YOU DON'T HAVE OR ARE
UNABLE TO ARTICULATE A PHILOSOPHY
OF YOUR OWN, YOU WILL INVARIABLY
INHERIT OR BE SUBJECT TO ADOPTING
SOMEBODY ELSE'S.
(26.09.2024)

WHENEVER YOU'RE LOOKING FOR
A PLACE TO LIVE/STAY IN,
"ENERGY ABUNDANCE" SHOULD BE
ONE OF YOUR TOP PRIORITIES.
IN ALL SENSES OF THE PHRASE.
(07.10.2024)

12. On the Masculine & Feminine

Men have to be independent, strong and decisive.

Women don't have to be independent, strong and decisive.

Women have to be with men who are strong, independent and decisive.

(09.02.2023)

With women, the Universe is quite strict.

"Oh, you still haven't conceived yet? Right. I see. Well then, bleed for me, bitch."

(01.05.2023)

WOMEN SHOULD NOT BE FORCED TO
WORRY ABOUT MONEY. THEY ARE ABOVE
THAT. WE ALL ACT AS IF THIS WAS ALL
NORMAL. LET ME ASSURE YOU, IT IS NOT.
IT'S THE MAN'S JOB TO PROTECT AND
PROVIDE. PERIOD. THE WOMAN'S TASK? I
DON'T KNOW, RAISE A FAMILY, MAKE A
HOME? BE AND CREATE BEAUTY AND
THROUGH THAT, BE THE GLUE THAT
HOLDS SOCIETIES TOGETHER? BE THE
FORCE THAT MAKES THE MEN GO OUT
THERE AND SOLVE PROBLEMS AND BUILD
STUFF AND FIGHT DEMONS. MAYBE?
(02.06.2023)

THE #1 THREAT TO SOCIETY ARE
WEAK MEN.
THE #2 THREAT TO SOCIETY ARE
EGOTISTICAL WOMEN.
(14.06.2023)

HE HAS TO BE STRONG SO
SHE COULD BE GENTLE.
THIS IS NOT JUST ABOUT THE
MAN/WOMAN RELATIONSHIP, BY THE
WAY. THIS IS ALSO THE GOD/EARTH
RELATIONSHIP, OR TO REPHRASE IT, THE
HUMANITY/EARTH RELATIONSHIP.
(22.07.2023)

MEN DON'T NEED THERAPY. MEN NEED
PHYSICAL EXERCISE AND/OR WORK.
PUSHUPS. PULLUPS. CHOPPING WOOD.
THEY ALSO NEED SOMEONE/SOMETHING
THEY'D BE WILLING TO DIE FOR. VALUES.
FAMILIES. PRINCIPLES.
WOMEN DON'T NEED THERAPY. WOMEN
NEED STRONG AND CAPABLE MEN TO
LEAD THEM AND SOMEONE/SOMETHING
TO TAKE CARE OF. CHILDREN.
HOUSEHOLDS. GARDENS. RESPECT THE
LAWS OF NATURE AND YOU WON'T NEED
MAN-MADE CONSTRUCTS TO SUPPORT
YOUR BEING.
(27.07.2023)

MEN PROTECT AND PROVIDE,
WOMEN SERVE AND CREATE.
(30.07.2023)

WHAT DO YOU DO WHEN A WOMAN
GHOSTS YOU? NOTHING. ABSOLUTELY
NOTHING. IF SHE DOESN'T RESPECT YOU
ENOUGH TO TAKE 2 MINUTES OF HER
TIME TO ANSWER YOU, SHE WILL NEVER
RESPECT YOU ENOUGH TO BE IN A
RELATIONSHIP WITH YOU, NOT TO
MENTION MARRIAGE OR CHILDREN. A
WOMAN IS SUPPOSED TO BE YOUR
BETTER HALF, MEANING SHE HAS TO
RESPECT YOU MORE THAN YOU RESPECT
YOURSELF.

ULTIMATELY, IF YOU ARE THE MAN THAT
YOU SAY YOU ARE, OR WANT TO BE, YOU
KNOW THAT IT'S HER LOSS, NOT YOURS.
(23.08.2023)

YOUR TOP PRIORITY AS A MAN IS TO SAVE YOUR GIRL FROM THE 9-5 SLAVERY, OR, IF POSSIBLE, TO MAKE SURE SHE'S NEVER FORCED INTO SUBMISSING HERSELF INTO IT IN THE FIRST PLACE. JUST MAKE SURE IT'S THE RIGHT GIRL.
(07.09.2023)

IF SHE DOESN'T HAVE THE UTMOST RESPECT FOR YOU, YOU'VE ALREADY LOST HER. BUT ALSO,
RESPECT IS EARNED, NOT GIVEN.
(21/23.09.2023)

DON'T CHASE. ATTRACT.
THAT ALSO APPLIES TO GIRLS.
(19.02.2024)

I MEAN, I AM A LEGITIMATE LOSER
MYSELF, YES, THAT IS DEFINITELY TRUE.
BUT WHENEVER I LOOK AROUND... AND
THE GUYS ARE, FOR LACK OF A BETTER
TERM, SPINELESS SIMPS. THEN REALLY I
CAN'T IMAGINE THE KIND OF VALLEY OF
DEATH THEY ARE CURRENTLY
MARCHING THROUGH, SPIRITUALLY.
THEN IT'S LIKE, NO WONDER THAT
ROMANCE IS DEAD.

(26.02.2024)

MOST OF THESE GIRLS DON'T WANT
YOU. THEY ONLY WANT YOUR
ATTENTION.

(18.04.2024)

I CANNOT HATE HER. IT'S ALL A
REFLECTION. THE MORE I HATE HER,
THE MORE I HATE MYSELF.

(19.05.2024)

MEN HAVE THIS INNATE NEED
FOR RESPECT.
BUT ALSO, THEY HAVE TO BE ABLE TO
EARN THAT RESPECT.
ONLY WHEN EARNED, IS RESPECT REAL.
OTHERWISE IT'S FAKE, AND IF IT'S FAKE,
THEN IT'S LIKE FAKE MONEY -
IT ENDS UP CORRUPTING THEM.
(15.06.2024)

THE MASCULINE RULES THE PHYSICAL
REALM;
THE FEMININE RULES THE SPIRITUAL
REALM.
(06.08.2024)

THE BIGGEST FEMINISTS IN THE WORLD
ARE MASCULINE MEN. BECAUSE THEY
ALLOW FOR THE WOMEN TO FULLY
EMBODY THEIR FEMININITY.

THE PROTECTING AND PROVIDING
FRAME OR FOUNDATION THEY SUPPLY
GIVES THE WOMEN THE SAFE
ENVIRONMENT TO BE FEMININE - TO BE
GENTLE, CARING, NURTURING, LOVING -
WITHOUT THE FEAR OF BEING TAKEN
ADVANTAGE OF AS A RESULT OF DOING
SO.

(08.09.2024)

13. On Failure & Disappointment

HAVING FAILED AS MANY TIMES AS I
HAVE, MY SUBSEQUENT CHANCES OF
SUCCESS ARE MUCH GREATER THAN OF
THOSE WHO HAVE NOT FAILED AT ALL.

(15.02.2023)

COMPLAIN ABOUT BEING BORED OR
NOT KNOWING WHAT TO DO AND YOU
WILL HAVE A SHITLOAD OF PROBLEMS
COMING YOUR WAY TO BE SOLVED.

DO YOU HAVE THE HUMILITY TO BE
GRATEFUL FOR THOSE PROBLEMS AND
TACKLE THEM WITH A CALM MIND OR
WILL YOU START STRESSING?

COMPLETELY UP TO YOU.

(27.04.2023)

SADNESS DOESN'T SOLVE ANYTHING.
THAT IS NOT TO SAY YOU SHOULD NOT
FEEL IT.

(28.04.2023)

MOST PROBLEMS ARE NOT
REALLY PROBLEMS AT ALL.
MOST PROBLEMS ARE JUST
DISTRACTIONS.

(15.06.2023)

DWELLING ON PAST MISTAKES IS A
MISTAKE. IGNORING PAST MISTAKES IS
AN EVEN BIGGER MISTAKE. THE ONLY
VIABLE OPTION IS TO LEARN FROM
THEM. LEARN AND LET GO. KNOW, BUT
LET GO. FORGIVE, BUT DON'T FORGET.
LIFE IS ABOUT GIVING (FORGIVING),
NOT GETTING (FORGETTING).

(07.08.2023)

I WOULD CALL MYSELF A PROFESSIONAL FAILURE. I FAIL AT MOST THINGS, AND I FAIL CONSTANTLY. PERHAPS THE ONLY DIFFERENCE BETWEEN ME AND MOST PEOPLE IS THAT I DON'T REVERT BACK TO THE "NORMAL," THE AVERAGE, THE SAFE, THE MEDIOCRE. I KEEP ON FAILIN'.

(18.08.2023)

THEY SAY THAT THE JOURNEY IS MORE IMPORTANT THAN THE DESTINATION.

WELL, MY DESTINATIONS HAVE MOSTLY BEEN FAILURES, BUT I SURE DID ENJOY THE JOURNEYS TO THOSE FAILURES, FOR WHAT IT'S WORTH.

(24.09.2023)

YOU CAN BE HARD ON YOURSELF
WITHOUT BEING HARSH ON YOURSELF.
DON'T CALL YOURSELF A FUCKTARD.
CALL YOURSELF A SILLY GOOSE. THE
MOST IMPORTANT THING IS TO NOT LIE.
EVERY LIE YOU TELL TO OTHERS
DESTRUCTS THE FABRIC OF SOCIETY AND
EVERY LIE YOU TELL YOURSELF
DESTRUCTS THE FABRIC OF YOUR SOUL.
IF YOU FUCKED UP, YOU FUCKED UP.
ONLY THAT YOU DIDN'T FUCK UP.

YOU MADE A ROOKIE MISTAKE.

(08/10.03.2024)

ALL YOUR MODELS ARE BROKEN.

ALL YOUR PLANS WILL FAIL.

ALL YOUR FRIENDS WILL PERISH.

PREPARE ACCORDINGLY.

(24.03.2024)

In order to become a winner
You must first admit
That you are a loser
Not only that, but also,
That the fact
Is solely, wholly and truly
Your fault
And no one else's.
(14/15.04.2024)

The assumption that every girl (or
guy) out there is out to hurt you,
is hurting you in and of itself.
(06.05.2024)

I know why you're scared, boy.
Yes, you don't really have a plan.
That's one thing. But the main
thing is that this is the "sink or
swim" moment. You're in deep.
(08.07.2024)

YOU CAN MAKE FRIENDS.

YOU CAN REVIVE OLD FRIENDSHIPS.

YOU CAN FIND LOVE.

YOU CAN GET TO THE TRUTH.

YOU CAN ALWAYS FIND GOD BY GOING WITHIN.

YOUR PAST MISTAKES DON'T DEFINE YOU.

YOUR FAILURES DON'T DEFINE YOU.

YOU CAN ALWAYS START ANEW.

(19.07.2024)

JUST WHEN YOU NEED THEM THE MOST, THEY ARE LIKELY TO TURN THEIR BACKS ON YOU.

DON'T LET THAT SURPRISE YOU.

(20.09.2024)

14. On Economics & Entrepreneurship

Bitcoin is the one consciousness,
the singularity of money.
(13.12.2022)

Money is Kung Fu.
Bitcoin is the Tao.
(03.02.2023)

We either have Bitcoin
or we have nothing.
(04.02.2023)

Fiat money is the main lever
of power the Kingdom of Death
has over us.
(06.02.2023)

WHEN YOU MEDITATE, YOU DON'T
THINK ABOUT MEDITATING.

IF YOU ARE SPIRITUAL, YOU DON'T
THINK ABOUT BEING SPIRITUAL. YOU
JUST ARE.

LIKEWISE, IF YOU HAVE MONEY, YOU
DON'T THINK ABOUT MONEY.

THAT'S HOW BITCOIN CHANGES ALL
INCENTIVES, THUS CHANGES US, THUS
CHANGES THE WORLD.

IT HELPS US VALUE THINGS THAT ARE
ACTUALLY VALUABLE.

(13.03.2023)

PRICE DOES NOT MEAN VALUE.
HOWEVER, PRICES AFFECT VALUES AND
VICE VERSA. THIS IS WHY, IN A WORLD
WHERE PRICES ARE DISTORTED, SO ARE
THE VALUES.

(24.03.2023)

IN THE FIAT SYSTEM, HISTORY WAS
WRITTEN BY THOSE WHO COULD LIE
BETTER. IN THE BITCOIN SYSTEM,
HISTORY IS BEING WRITTEN BY THOSE
WHO TELL THE TRUTH BETTER.
(31.03.2023)

THROUGH BITCOIN, WE HAVE GOD IN
MONEY. IT HAS BECOME HOLY.
(31.03.2023)

THERE'S THE SAYING THAT EVERYTHING
IS GOOD FOR BITCOIN. THAT IS TRUE.
AS IS TRUE THAT EVERYTHING IS GOOD
FOR ME.
(08.04.2023)

INFLATION IS NOT A REQUIREMENT FOR
A SUSTAINABLE ECONOMY.
INFLATION IS A REQUIREMENT FOR
AN UNSUSTAINABLE ECONOMY.
(12.04.2023)

BITCOIN AS THE NETWORK IS GOOD FOR THE ENVIRONMENT BECAUSE IT INCENTIVIZES EFFICIENCY.

BITCOIN AS THE ASSET IS GOOD FOR THE ENVIRONMENT AS IT ALLOWS FOR THESE EFFICIENCY GAINS TO BE STORED AND MOVED THROUGH SPACE AND TIME IN A THERMODYNAMICALLY SECURE MANNER, WHILE ALSO REWARDING OTHERS FOR PARTICIPATING IN THAT SYSTEM.
(20/22.04.2023)

BITCOIN REBUILT AND REIMAGINED THE INSTITUTION OF MONEY, WHICH IS THE BASE ENERGY OF THE ECONOMY, WHICH IS THE BASE ENERGY OF SOCIETY. ALL OTHER INSTITUTIONS ALSO MUST BE REBUILT, UNDER A BITCOIN STANDARD.
(25.04.2023)

At some point in the near future, a central bank will start printing money with the purpose of buying Bitcoin. Once they start, there will be no incentive for them to stop. That's when your HODL game has to be the strongest. Because if you start realizing your paper gains then you may realize that the realized gains were the real paper gains all along. The other problem is that a central bank has no incentive to announce that they have started acquiring Bitcoin. For that, we will probably have to rely on whistleblowers, on-chain analysis and uncensorable communication protocols such as the Bitcoin network itself, nostr and other similar solutions.

(25.04.2023)

ONE OF THE MAIN THINGS I'M TRYING TO CONVEY IS THAT UNDERSTANDING BITCOIN IS PARAMOUNT TO YOUR SUCCESS IN THE WORLD WE ARE MOVING INTO. AND NOT JUST IN TERMS OF BEING ABLE TO INCREASE YOUR OWN ECONOMIC ABILITY, MOBILITY AND FREEDOM, BUT ALSO, AND MORE IMPORTANTLY, IN UNDERSTANDING THE MECHANICS OF OUR REALITY IN GENERAL. BECAUSE I DO TRULY BELIEVE THAT ONCE YOU UNDERSTAND HOW BITCOIN WORKS, YOU CAN UNDERSTAND HOW EVERYTHING WORKS. BUT I ALSO KNOW THAT NONE OF US REALLY KNOWS YET HOW BITCOIN WORKS. AND WHY IT IS SO EASY TO MAKE THAT CLAIM IS SIMPLY BECAUSE WE ARE SO EARLY. WE'VE LIVED MOST OF OUR LIVES ON A FIAT STANDARD. HELL, WE'RE STILL LIVING MOST OF OUR LIVES ON A FIAT STANDARD, EVEN THE BITCOINERS.

WE STILL DENOMINATE IN FIAT, PAY FOR
OUR GROCERIES IN FIAT. WE MAY KNOW
HOW BITCOIN WORKS ON A TECHNICAL
LEVEL, AND TO AN EXTENT, HOW IT
WORKS ON THE ECONOMIC LEVEL. BUT
ON A MENTAL LEVEL? SPIRITUAL LEVEL?
SOCIETAL LEVEL? MAN. WE HAVE NO
CLUE. AND THAT'S A HUGE PART OF WHY
IT ALL EXCITES ME SO MUCH. WE CAN
LITERALLY FUCK AROUND AND FIND
OUT. WE ARE THE TRAILBLAZERS. WE ARE
THE VISIONARIES.

(08.05.2023)

WHAT IS BITCOIN? BITCOIN IS A TOOL
THAT ENABLES US TO REALIZE OUR
HIGHEST POTENTIAL AS A SPECIES.

(12.05.2023)

A "BUSINESS PLAN" AS A CONCEPT IS
REDUNDANT. THERE'S THE BUSINESS
IDEA, AND THE EXECUTION OF THE IDEA.
BOTH OF WHICH REQUIRE A CERTAIN
DEGREE OF ELASTICITY TO BE ABLE TO
ADAPT TO THE CONSTANTLY CHANGING
MARKET CONDITIONS AKA REALITY. THE
"PLAN" MUST CHANGE AND EVOLVE IN
TANDEM WITH THE MARKET.
(14.05.2023)

CHOOSING BITCOIN IS
PREDOMINANTLY A MORAL IMPERATIVE.
ALL OTHER FORMS OF MONEY
(THAT WE KNOW OF) ARE PRONE TO
CENTRALIZATION, WHICH MEANS THEY
ARE PRONE TO CORRUPTION, WHICH
MEANS THEY ARE INHERENTLY IMMORAL.
(19.05/23.06.2023)

BITCOIN IS A BATTERY OF
EVER-EXPANDING ENCRYPTED ENERGY
IN CYBERSPACE.
(21.05.2023)

CHOOSE FIAT AND YOU ARE
CHOOSING THE SYSTEM OF DEATH.
CHOOSE BITCOIN AND YOU ARE
CHOOSING THE SYSTEM OF LIFE.
IT REALLY IS THAT BIG OF A DEAL
AND IT REALLY IS BINARY.
(21.05.2023)

PROOF OF STAKE MIMICS FIAT MONEY.
PROOF OF WORK MIMICS COMMODITY
MONEY.
THAT'S ALL YOU REALLY NEED TO KNOW
TO MAKE AN INFORMED DECISION.
(23.05.2023)

STUDY BITCOIN.

LOOK INTO WHAT IT IS AND
HOW IT WORKS.

THEN TAKE THOSE PERSPECTIVES
AND APPLY THE SAME PRINCIPLES
TO EVERYTHING ELSE.

(26.05.2023)

YOUR NUMBER 1 PRIORITY IS NOT
TO MAKE PROFIT.

IT'S TO PROVIDE VALUE.

(30.05.2023)

THE NOTION OF SCARCITY IN TERMS OF
THE BITCOIN BLOCKSPACE IS A BIT OF A
PARADOX, ISN'T IT? IT IS SCARCE, BUT
THE SCARCITY IS ACTUALLY ENFORCED
BY TIME, IN THE FORM OF WHAT
SATOSHI CALLED THE TIMECHAIN AND
THE 10 MINUTE BLOCK INTERVALS.

THE DATA THAT PASSES THIS FILTER,
THIS GATE OF COSTLINESS, AND IS
INCLUDED IN A BLOCK, ALL OF A
SUDDEN ACTUALLY BECOMES
INCREASINGLY ABUNDANT IN BOTH
SPACE AND TIME, FOREVER, AS IT IS
EMBEDDED INTO EVERY PRESENT AND
FUTURE FULL NODE IN THE NETWORK.

(05.06.2023)

HERE'S ANOTHER REASON WHY BITCOIN
IS BOUND TO HAVE RELIGIOUS
IMPLICATIONS:
IT WILL LITERALLY SAVE PEOPLE'S LIVES,
THEIR FAMILIES, THEIR BUSINESSES.
OBVIOUSLY PEOPLE WILL BE ETERNALLY
GRATEFUL FOR THAT, AND THEY WILL
WANT TO DISPLAY THAT GRATITUDE,
THAT SENSE OF INDEBTEDNESS.
THE RESULT CANNOT BE ANY DIFFERENT
FROM A RELIGIOUS MOVEMENT.
(08.06.2023)

FIAT MONEY BECOMES
WORTH LESS OVER THE MEDIUM TERM,
WORTHLESS OVER THE LONG TERM.
STUDY BITCOIN.
(11.06.2023)

2 STEPS TO VICTORY:

1. GET OFF ZERO (BITCOIN)

2. GET ON ZERO (FIAT)

(23.06.2023)

BITCOIN IS NOT A CULT,

IT'S A CULTURE.

(29.06.2023)

BITCOIN IS THE IMMEASURABLE.

EVERYTHING DIVIDED BY 21 MILLION

IS IMMEASURABLE.

(29.06.2023)

I DON'T LIKE TO CHEER ON THE DEMISE
OF THE FIAT SYSTEM AS A PRINCIPLE.
I DON'T THINK IT'S MORAL TO CHEER
ON SOMETHING THAT'S GOING TO
BRING WITH IT DEATH AND
DESTRUCTION.
HOWEVER, IT IS PAINFULLY CLEAR THAT
SOME PEOPLE DON'T LEARN
ANY OTHER WAY.
AND FOR WHAT IT'S WORTH:
BETTER A PAINFUL END
THAN ENDLESS PAIN.
(07.07.2023)

BITCOIN HAS THE POTENTIAL TO BE
THE BIGGEST, MOST TRANSFORMATIVE
SPIRITUAL REVOLUTION MANKIND
HAS EVER WITNESSED, SIMPLY DUE TO
THE FACT THAT IT IS EXPLICITLY NOT
A SPIRITUAL REVOLUTION,
BUT AN ECONOMIC/PHYSICAL
(FINANCIAL FREEDOM)
AND A MENTAL
(FREEDOM OF THOUGHT & SPEECH)
REVOLUTION FIRST AND FOREMOST.
THE SPIRITUAL (LOVE) REVOLUTION
IS DOWNSTREAM FROM THESE
FOUNDATIONAL LAYERS.
(24.07.2023)

THE STATES THAT HAVE BEEN
PORTRAYING THEMSELVES AS CAPITALIST,
WHEN INDEED THEY ARE COMMUNIST,
WILL HAVE TO FACE TWO FUNDAMENTAL
TRUTHS:

1. FREE MARKET CAPITALISM
OUTCOMPETES COMMUNISM IN THE
LONG TERM

2. WE, THE PEOPLE, NOW HAVE THE
TECHNOLOGICAL PROWESS TO OPT OUT
OF THIS SYSTEM OF GLOBAL
COMMUNISM AND OPT IN TO A SYSTEM
OF REAL CAPITALISM

(15/17.08.2023)

MONEY IS AN EXTREMELY
PHILOSOPHICAL TOPIC AS IT'S ONE OF
THOSE THINGS THAT COORDINATES
HUMAN ACTION ON A LARGE SCALE.

(17.09.2023)

BITCOIN CONSUMES ENERGY IN ORDER TO EMPOWER THE HUMAN SPIRIT. IT IS THE GREATEST HUMANITARIAN INVENTION EVER CONCEIVED.

(21.09.2023)

DUE TO OUR INDEBTEDNESS TO BOTH BITCOIN AND HUMANITY, WE FEEL THE CALLING TO SPREAD THE KNOWLEDGE, EFFECTIVELY BECOMING A FREE MARKETING TEAM FOR THE BITCOIN BRAND. THIS IS GRATITUDE AS A FORCE OF ACTION, IN ACTION.

(05.10.2023)

I THINK IT'S IMPORTANT TO UNDERSTAND THAT AT THE ROOT OF IT, MOST OF THE EVIL PREVALENT IN THE WORLD TODAY STEMS FROM 2 SYSTEMS: THE MILITARY-INDUSTRIAL COMPLEX AND THE STATE-FINANCIAL COMPLEX. AND THAT AT THE CRUX OF IT IS THE EVER-EXPANDING SYNERGY BETWEEN THOSE 2 SYSTEMS, WHICH LEAD TO ONLY 2 CERTAIN OUTCOMES: BIGGER STATES AND MORE WARS. LUCKILY, WE HAVE MORE AND MORE OPTIONS TO OPT OUT OF THOSE SYSTEMS.

BITCOIN FIXES (SOME OF) THIS.

(15.10.2023)

BITCOIN IS THE CURRENCY OF LOVE, PEACE AND COOPERATION AS IT MAKES VIOLENCE UNPROFITABLE.

(21.10.2023)

THERE SHOULD BE A SYNERGY BETWEEN
DOING YOUR "WORK" AND WORKING ON
YOURSELF.
(26.10.2023)

BITCOIN IS AN IMPORTANT PIECE
OF THE PUZZLE. IF YOU DON'T GET IT,
YOU'RE NOT GETTING THE FULL PICTURE.
STAY HUMBLE, STUDY BITCOIN.
(26.12.2023)

DEFLATION = GOOD; GENERALLY THE
NATURAL STATE OF THE FREE MARKET
DEFLATION IN A SYSTEM THAT REQUIRES
INFLATION TO EXIST IN ORDER TO
FUNCTION = BAD
(21.02.2024)

THREE STEPS TO A PROSPEROUS LIFE:

1. STUDY BITCOIN

2. TEACH YOUR KIDS ABOUT BITCOIN

3. STAY HUMBLE

(22.02.2024)

ULTIMATELY, WHAT BITCOIN REPRESENTS IS A TRANSFER OF WEALTH AND POWER FROM THE POLITICAL/CANTILLIONAIRE CLASS TO THE FREE MARKET. THUS, MANY POLITICIANS (NOT TO MENTION BANKERS AND ESPECIALLY CENTRAL BANKERS) TEND TO OPPOSE THE VERY NOTION OF A ROGUE MONEY SUCH AS BITCOIN, AND RIGHTLY SO, AS THE WHOLE PREMISE IS ANTITHETICAL TO THEIR VERY BEING, AND MOST OF THEM WILL BE MADE OBSOLETE.

(22.02.2024)

FIAT MONEY WILL BE REGARDED AS THE BIGGEST AND MOST DESTRUCTIVE SCAM IN HUMAN HISTORY.

(29.02.2024)

OWN A POSITIVE CASH FLOW BEFORE YOU OWN BITCOIN.

OTHERWISE YOU ARE NOT HOLDING ONTO THE MOST PRISTINE ASSET AND THE FUTURE OF MONEY, BUT A LOTTERY TICKET. TO AN EXTENT, AT THIS STAGE OF ITS EVOLUTION, BTC IS A LOTTERY TICKET... WITH INCREASING ODDS OF WINNING THE LONGER YOU HODL.

POSITIVE SATS FLOW IS ULTIMATELY THE NAME OF THE GAME

FIAT MONEY IS ALSO A LOTTERY TICKET... GUARANTEED TO LOSE ITS VALUE OVER TIME (EXCEPT FOR IN A DEFLATIONARY ENVIRONMENT), WITH INCREASING ODDS OF LOSING THE LONGER YOU HODL.

(29.02.2024)

"THE MARKET CAN REMAIN IRRATIONAL
LONGER THAN YOU CAN REMAIN
SOLVENT."

THAT IS ESPECIALLY TRUE IN THE FIAT
WORLD. ALSO, AS A FIAT MONEY
APPROACHES THE END OF ITS LIFE AND
HYPERINFLATION, AN INCREASE OF
VOLATILITY IN ASSET PRICES IS TO BE
EXPECTED (SEE: WEIMAR GERMANY).
(29.02.2024)

CONTROL OVER THE MONEY PRINTER IS
THE MOST IMPORTANT TOOL IN
ESTABLISHING AND MAINTAINING
A COMMUNIST REGIME.
FEW.
(29.02.2024)

When you control the money,

then you control the economy;

when you control the economy,

then you control the incentives;

when you control the incentives,

then you control the minds;

when you control the minds,

then you control the will;

when you control the will,

then you control the spirit.

Because ultimately, it is the will of

the spirit that allows for things

to happen or not to happen.

(01.03.2024)

BITCOIN IS THE MOST POWERFUL
RELIGION BECAUSE IT ENTAILS IN ITSELF
SUCH AN IMMENSE, TANGIBLE AND
SEEMINGLY EVER-EXPANDING WEALTH
THAT SIMPLY CANNOT BE ARGUED AWAY.
IT IS THE PRAGMATIC STATIST'S WORST
NIGHTMARE.
(10.03.2024)

IN A WORLD THAT'S BUILT UPON LIE$
ßEING TRUTHFUL IS THE ULTIMATE ACT
OF REBELLION
(10.03.2024)

THE POINT FOR ME, WHEN I GOT SORT
OF RADICALIZED AND VOCAL ABOUT
BITCOIN WAS WHEN I REALIZED THAT
THERE IS A HIGH PROBABILITY THAT
BITCOIN IS NOT ONLY AN ALTERNATIVE,
BUT PERHAPS THE ONLY HOPE.
(15.03.2024)

Bitcoin is NgU technology as in:
"Number go Up technology"
on a monetary level.
"Never give Up technology"
on a mental level.
(16.03.2024)

Bitcoin is an empire without an
emperor and without borders.
(17.03.2024)

It's amazing how many of these
macro dudes are like:
"Yeah, there's a high probability of
a global recession, but not to
worry, the Fed is going to have to
step in with QE and the money
printer so all is going to be just
fine."
It's like... how naive can you be?
The money printer only works
until the revolutions start.
(17.03.2024)

WHEN YOU GET INTO BITCOIN,
THE PRICE IS THE MOST EXCITING
THING ABOUT IT.
WHEN YOU GET BITCOIN,
THE PRICE IS THE LEAST EXCITING
THING ABOUT IT.
(11.04.2024)

WHAT WILL HAPPEN WHEN A WHOLE
GENERATION OF YOUNG PEOPLE WAKES
UP TO THE FACT THAT NOT ONLY HAVE
THEY BEEN ROBBED OF THE FRUITS OF
THEIR LABOR, BUT ALSO OF THEIR
HEALTH, CHILDREN, FAMILY,
COMMUNITY, GOD/SPIRITUALITY
AND THE ABILITY TO REDEEM
THEMSELVES? WILL HUMANITY SURVIVE
THE UPHEAVAL?

THE FLIPSIDE OF THIS IS - IF THERE'S NO
UPHEAVAL, WE ARE DOOMED ANYWAY.
BITCOIN IS THE WAY TO MAKE THAT
UPHEAVAL A PEACEFUL ONE - SIMPLY BY
MAKING THINGS OBSOLETE, AS OPPOSED
TO DESTROYING THEM.
(07.05.2024)

WEAK MONEY, WEAK PEOPLE,
WEAK MORALS = HARD TIMES.
SOUND MONEY, SOUND PEOPLE,
SOUND MORALS = GOOD TIMES.
(13.05.2024)

A GOOD INDICATION OF HOW UPSIDE DOWN THE WORLD WE LIVE IN TODAY IS, IS HOW WORDS LIKE "AMBITION" AND "SUCCESS" HAVE GOTTEN A NEGATIVE CONNOTATION. SIMILARLY, "PROFIT" IS BEING SEEN AS "VALUE RETRACTED" OR "VALUE STOLEN" EVEN, AND NOT "VALUE ADDED," WHICH IS WHAT IT SHOULD REALLY MEAN.

(22.03.2023/14.05.2024)

THE SINGLE BEST THING A GOVERNMENT CAN DO FOR ITS ECONOMY IS TO STAY OUT OF IT.

(26.05.2024)

I DO THINK THE PRODUCTIVITY GAINS
FROM AI + ROBOTICS ARE REAL,
REMARKABLE AND COMPOUNDING.

BUT ME, PERSONALLY? I'M STILL WAY
MORE EXCITED ABOUT THE ENERGY
ABUNDANCE AND SUBSEQUENT
PRODUCTIVITY GAINS THAT BITCOIN
MINING IS BOUND TO UNLEASH ON THE
WORLD.

(13.06.2024)

YOU TRADE BITCOIN
FOR THE DOLLAR GAINS.
I SAVE IN BITCOIN
FOR THE WORLD TO CHANGE.
WE ARE NOT THE SAME.

(25.06.2024)

Cash flow (sats flow) is
the most important. Out of assets,
it is only Bitcoin that's real.
It also IS cash flow, in a sense.
It pays a dividend on the yield
of humanity.
(04.07.2024)

When banking works,
it's very convenient.
When it doesn't, you're fucked.
Bitcoin fixes this.
(11.07.2024)

Self-custodying Bitcoin is the
real...
Occupy Wall Street
End the Fed
Power to the People
(16.07.2024)

THE AIR THAT WE BREATHE IS THE MOST
VALUABLE THING IN THE WORLD. LIFE
CANNOT EXIST WITHOUT AIR, WITHOUT
BREATH. HOWEVER, AS AIR IS
EVERYWHERE, IT IS ABUNDANT, WE DO
NOT ASSIGN A "PRICE" TO AIR (UNDER
NORMAL CIRCUMSTANCES). I THINK
THIS IS WHAT BITCOIN WILL GRADUALLY
DO TO ENERGY. IT MAKES IT MORE
ABUNDANT, WHICH IN TURN MAKES IT
CHEAPER, UNTIL IT REACHES A PRICE OF
NEAR ZERO. AND SINCE ENERGY IS THE
MAIN INPUT TO EVERYTHING WE
PRODUCE, THE ABUNDANCE SPILLS OVER
TO EVERYTHING ELSE IT TOUCHES.

(28.07.2024)

CAPITALISM IS THE CREATION OF VALUE.
SOCIALISM IS THE REDISTRIBUTION OF
VALUE. I THINK IT'S QUITE EVIDENT
WHICH ONE IS A NET BENEFIT AND
WHICH ONE IS A NET NEGATIVE.

(10.08.2024)

THE WORLD IS ADDICTED TO ALCOHOL,
TO SUGAR, TO OPIOIDS... BUT ABOVE ALL,
IT'S ADDICTED TO CHEAP CREDIT. IT'S
ADDICTED TO BORROWING FROM
FUTURE GENERATIONS IN ORDER TO PAY
FOR THE STUPIDITY OF OURSELVES AND
OUR ANCESTORS. NOTHING WILL
CHANGE UNTIL WE START LIVING FOR
THE FUTURE, NOT FROM THE FUTURE.

(18.08.2024)

FIATNAM (NOUN) - AN ECONOMIC,
MENTAL AND SPIRITUAL WARFARE
WAGED BY THE PARASITIC CLASS
AGAINST THE PRODUCTIVE CLASS.

(29.08.2024)

PEOPLE CONFLATE "HAVING A JOB" AND "WORKING." MOST PEOPLE WHO HAVE A JOB HAVE IT BECAUSE THEY NEED TO PAY THE BILLS. MOST PEOPLE WHO ACTUALLY WORK DO IT BECAUSE THEY CANNOT NOT DO IT. THE WORD "PROFESSION" IN ESTONIAN IS "ELUKUTSE" WHICH LITERALLY TRANSLATES TO "LIFE'S CALLING" AND SIMILARLY, THE ENGLISH WORD "VOCATION" COMES FROM THE LATIN VERB VOCĀRE - MEANING "TO CALL" - WHICH IS WHAT WORK SHOULD BE ALL ABOUT. IT **SHOULD BE A CALLING.** ALSO, PEOPLE LIKE TO DEFINE THEMSELVES VIA THEIR JOB - IT'S QUITE WIDESPREAD IN THE CULTURE - WHEN YOU MEET SOMEONE, ONE OF THE FIRST THINGS THEY ASK IS QUITE OFTEN "WHAT DO YOU DO FOR A LIVING?" SOME PEOPLE (OR PERHAPS MOST PEOPLE?) HAVEN'T TRULY FOUND THEMSELVES SO THEY THINK WHAT THEY DO IS WHO THEY ARE...

(06.09.2024)

THE CURRENT MONETARY SYSTEM IS A
PONZI SCHEME. BUT IT'S NOT A PONZI
SCHEME IN THE SENSE THAT IT NEEDS
MORE PEOPLE JOINING IT IN ORDER TO
CONTINUE (ALTHOUGH A LACK OF
PEOPLE CAN BE A BIG PROBLEM AS
DEMONSTRATED BY CHINA AND JAPAN
IN REAL TIME). WHAT IT NEEDS, IN
ORDER TO NOT COLLAPSE, IS MORE
UNITS OF THE CURRENCY. BECAUSE THE
VAST MAJORITY OF MONEY IN EXISTENCE
TODAY IS DEBT - IT'S OWED BY
SOMEONE, TO SOMEONE. WHAT DEBT
HAS IS **INTEREST**. THERE ALWAYS NEEDS
TO BE MORE NEW MONEY TO PAY FOR
THE OLD MONEY. IF THE MONEY
GROWTH SLOWS DOWN OR GOES
NEGATIVE (LESS DEBT/MONEY IS
CREATED THAN IS REPAID) FOR AN
EXTENDED PERIOD OF TIME, THERE WILL
SIMPLY NOT BE ENOUGH MONEY IN
EXISTENCE IN ORDER TO FULFILL THE
CLAIMS ON THE MONEY.

THIS IS WHY DEFLATION IS NOT ONLY INCOMPATIBLE WITH THE CURRENT FINANCIAL SYSTEM; IT'S **THE BIGGEST THREAT** TO IT.

(09/10.09.2024)

STARTING A BUSINESS IS ALSO VERY MUCH ABOUT OVERCOMING ALL SORTS OF FEARS: FEAR OF FAILURE, OF COMMITMENT, OF BUREAUCRACY, OF PEOPLE, OF ROUTINE, OF BECOMING A SLAVE TO YOUR OWN SYSTEM.

(02.10.2024)

TALKING ABOUT A POTENTIAL "FINANCIAL CRISIS" IS A BIT OF A MISNOMER SINCE THE FINANCIAL SYSTEM IS A CRISIS IN AND OF ITSELF.

(04.10.2024)

WHEN YOU EMBARK ON
ENTREPRENEURSHIP,
YOU "ADD VENTURE,"
WHICH IT LITERALLY IS -
AN ADVENTURE.
(06.10.2024)

15. On Expectations

DO NOT EXPECT TO KNOW EVERYTHING.
EXPECT TO KNOW NOTHING
AND TO BE PROVEN WRONG.
(05.12.2022)

YOU ARE PROJECTING.
AND BY PROJECTING, YOU'RE EXPECTING.
DROP IT. DON'T PREDICT.
DON'T EXTRAPOLATE.
STAY IN THE NOW.
(26.03.2023)

IF I ACCIDENTALLY TEACH SOMEONE
SOMETHING, THEN THAT'S EXTRA.
(08.04.2023)

As always, it's my expectations that
hurt me the most.
I expect things, that's the first
mistake.
It's also that I expect too much
and too fast.
But mostly, it's that I expect.
(19.06.2023)

The absurdity of "lack" as a concept
is just too funny.
(20.06.2023)

Nobody gets it. Nobody believes
in you. No one even cares.
That alone should be enough of a
motivation to do it.
Do it for the love
and do it out of spite.
They are not mutually exclusive.
(19.08.2023)

Don't expect to be useful.
Or known. Or celebrated.
Or noticed. You're a nobody.
You're not entitled to anything.
(04.01.2024)

You can tell how insecure a person
is by the amount of credentials
and achievements they list when
introducing themselves. Since they
define themselves via these
external metrics, they also tend to
be more rigid in their worldviews,
more arrogant, and less likely to
honestly and intellectually
consider alternative ideas.
(22.05.2024)

NO ONE CAN LET ME DOWN.

IT IS ONLY I WHO CAN LET ME DOWN.

ANYBODY ELSE LETTING ME DOWN IS A
MISNOMER, BECAUSE THEN, TOO, IT WAS
I WHO LET MYSELF DOWN BY HAVING
EXPECTATIONS REGARDING THINGS
THAT ARE OUTSIDE OF MY CONTROL.
(08.08.2024)

YOU GET EXACTLY WHAT YOU NEED.

NO MORE, NO LESS.

(29.08.2024)

TRY TO DO EVERYTHING
AND YOU END UP DOING NOTHING.
(04.10.2024)

Your only real problem is
your expectations.
Your reliance on the outcome.
Your cravings for validation.
(09.10.2024)

Everyone's corruptible.
Remember that.
(03.11.2024)

16. On Community & Isolation

NONE OF US ARE MEANT TO DO IT
ALONE.

(25.12.2022)

FIND YOUR TRIBE.

(16.01.2023)

BELONGING THROUGH CONFORMING
IS FAKE BELONGING.

(09.06.2023)

DON'T EXPEND YOUR ENERGY ON
PEOPLE WHO DON'T VALUE IT.
THERE ARE PLENTY WHO WILL.

(01.07.2023)

SOCIAL MEDIA WILL NOT CURE
LONELINESS. LIKES ARE NOT LOVE;
FOLLOWERS ARE NOT FAMILY AND
FRIENDS; INFORMATION IS NOT
INTEGRATION.
(09.07.2023)

I DO ENJOY SOLITUDE.
LONELINESS - NOT SO MUCH.
(14.07.2023)

THE THING WITH RELATIONSHIPS...
IS LIKE WITH EVERYTHING ELSE.
QUALITY OVER QUANTITY.
REALNESS OVER FAKENESS.
(21.08.2023)

THE THING ABOUT LONELINESS, NOT
FITTING IN, NOT FINDING LOVE - ON
THE HERO'S JOURNEY - IS DEFINITELY A
REAL AND DIFFICULT PART OF IT.

PERHAPS EVEN WORSE, THOUGH, IS THE
FEELING OF HAVING SO MUCH TO OFFER
TO THE WORLD, AND THE WORLD
SIMPLY NOT WANTING IT.

THE ULTIMATE REJECTION.

(08.11.2023)

WE ALL CARRY WITHIN OURSELVES
THESE DEEP DARK PITS OF ABSOLUTE
LONELINESS AND WE'RE REALLY JUST
TRYING TO FIND THE RIGHT PEOPLE TO
DISTRACT US FROM THE FACT.

(11.02.2024)

MOST OF SOCIETY ARE HERD ANIMALS,
SO YOU CAN'T REALLY EXPECT THEM TO
FOLLOW A LONE WOLF - OR TO EVEN
UNDERSTAND ONE.

(15.02.2024)

I FOOLED MYSELF INTO THINKING
PEOPLE CARED FOR ME.
THEY DON'T.
I NEED TO CARE FOR MYSELF.
(16.02.2024)

I GUESS I ALWAYS KNEW I DIDN'T FIT IN.
MAYBE THAT'S WHY I WENT
INTROVERTED - TO ACT AS IF
MY LONELINESS WAS MY CHOICE.
(23.02.2024)

THE MONEY IS NOT GOING TO
MEAN ANYTHING WITHOUT THE PEOPLE.
(05.03.2024)

IF YOU'RE NUMBER ONE,
YOU'LL ALWAYS BE ALONE.
HENCE THE NUMBER.
(28.04.2024)

PEOPLE DON'T GATHER AROUND YOU
WHEN YOU NEED THEM. PEOPLE GATHER
AROUND YOU WHEN THEY NEED YOU.

THIS IS WHY THE POLITICAL CLASS
AROUND THE WORLD TODAY CAN'T BE
REALLY CALLED "LEADERS."

THEY NEED THE PEOPLE AROUND THEM
TO GIVE THEM VALIDITY.

ACTUAL LEADERS ARE ALREADY VALID
AND PEOPLE WILL GATHER AROUND
THEM BECAUSE OF THAT.

(03.05.2024)

I YEARNED FOR DIALOGUE.

I TURNED TO MY FRIENDS.

I DIDN'T GET IT.

I TURNED TO SOCIAL MEDIA.

I DIDN'T GET IT.

NOW, I MUST TURN TO THE GODS.

(19.05.2024)

IF BEING TRUE TO WHO YOU ARE MEANS
YOU LOSE SOME FRIENDS, LET THEM GO.
THEY WERE NEVER REALLY YOUR
FRIENDS IN THE FIRST PLACE.
(30.05.2024)

I DON'T REALLY HAVE ANY FRIENDS.
AT THE SAME TIME, I CONSIDER
EVERYBODY MY FRIEND, BECAUSE
WHETHER WE LIKE IT OR NOT, WE ARE
ONE BIG FAMILY. WE CAME FROM THE
SAME PLACE AND WE GO BACK TO THE
SAME PLACE WHEN WE ARE FINISHED.
(13.07.2024)

IT'S ABOUT THE COMPROMISE BETWEEN:

- KNOWING YOU NEED TO BE OK
  WITH BEING ALONE
- KNOWING RELATIONSHIPS ARE
  THE MOST IMPORTANT THING IN
  LIFE

(19.07.2024)

Treat every person as if they were the key to unlocking the next level of your personal journey. Because they just might be.
(20.08.2024)

Don't let your loneliness dictate how and who you spend your time with.
(23.08.2024)

We have been sold the following slogan: "You can do anything." It's one of those things that's both true and untrue at the same time. The thing is, the saying doesn't capture the nuance, the contexts in which the statement is true or not.

IN THE GRAND SCHEME OF THINGS, YES,
MANKIND IS ALL-POWERFUL IN A VERY
REAL SENSE, AND WE CAN DO ALMOST
ANYTHING WE SET OUR MINDS TO.
HOWEVER, HERE'S THE NUANCE. IT'S THE
"WE," NOT JUST "YOU." SURE, YOU ARE
THE MASTER OF YOUR FATE. YOU CREATE
YOUR CHARACTER. BUT HAVE YOU EVER
TRIED TO BUILD A PENCIL FROM
SCRATCH? HAVE YOU EVER TRIED TO
FEED YOURSELF ON FOOD THAT YOU
ONLY GREW YOURSELF?

(04.09.2024)

I DESPISE MY LONELINESS,

YET YEARN FOR SOLITUDE.

WHAT AN ODD AND

CONFUSING COMBINATION.

(12.09.2024)

I THINK ONE OF THE MAIN REASONS
WHY I DON'T REALLY GO OUT A LOT IS
BECAUSE I'M PRONE TO FALLING FOR
ANY AND EVERY BEAUTIFUL GIRL THERE
IS. AND I ALSO KNOW NO ONE'S EVER
REALLY FALLEN FOR ME. SO IN A SENSE,
EVERY GORGEOUS FACE I SEE BECOMES A
SOURCE OF HEARTBREAK.

(19.09.2024)

FROM LONELINESS TO HOLINESS.

(12.10.2024)

JUST LIKE THERE ARE PEOPLE THAT I
WANT TO HELP, AND CAN HELP;
THERE ARE PEOPLE THAT WANT TO,
AND CAN, HELP ME.

(16.10.2024)

17. On Feelings

DON'T QUESTION

THE NATURE OF REALITY.

DON'T QUESTION

WHAT YOU FEEL.

IT IS REAL.

AS REAL AS ANYTHING.

(25.12.2022)

I WAS LOOKING FOR CLARITY.

ALL I GOT WAS FEELINGS.

(28.12.2022)

ONCE YOU LEARN HOW TO FEEL
EVERYTHING, YOU WILL FEEL
EVERYTHING. THE GOOD AND THE BAD.
AND THE NUMBING WON'T WORK
ANYMORE. THE SUPPRESSION WON'T
WORK ANYMORE. EVERYTHING THAT'S
THERE WILL BE PUT IN THE SPOTLIGHT
AND IT CAN'T BE TURNED OFF UNTIL
YOU'VE DEALT WITH IT. AND "DEALING
WITH IT" CAN BE A LIFELONG JOURNEY.
SO YOU GOTTA BE READY FOR THAT.
ACCEPT THAT.

(01.01.2023)

I THOUGHT I'VE SOWN
THE SEEDS OF PERFECTION.
BUT THEY WERE REALLY
THE SEEDS OF REJECTION.

(01.01.2023)

NO RULES. JUST INTUITION.

(09.05.2023)

IF YOU ARE RIGHT, AND YOU HAVE THE
ARGUMENTS OR EXPERIENCE TO
SUPPORT IT, THERE IS ABSOLUTELY NO
REASON TO GET ANGRY OR EMOTIONAL
WHEN SOMEONE DISAGREES WITH YOU.
(21.05.2023)

I'M NOT TRYING TO BE THE BEST
I'M JUST TRYING TO HATE MYSELF
A LITTLE LESS
(02.12.2023)

CRYING IS NOT NECESSARILY
A SIGN OF WEAKNESS.
MOSTLY, IT'S A SIGN OF WILLINGNESS
TO ACKNOWLEDGE YOUR FEELINGS
AND TO LET GO.
(23.02.2024)

I DON'T ONLY WANT TO BE TRUSTED,
I ALSO WANT TO TRUST.
(26.06.2024)

IF YOU ASK ME, SENSITIVITY IS ONE OF
THE GREATEST GIFTS A HUMAN BEING
CAN BE BLESSED WITH.
BUT IT'S ALSO ONE OF THE BIGGEST
RESPONSIBILITIES AND
HEAVIEST BURDENS.
MAKE NO MISTAKE THOUGH,
IT IS A GIFT.
IN ORDER TO FULLY UTILIZE IT,
YOU MUST BE VULNERABLE,
BUT ANTIFRAGILE.
OPEN, BUT SELECTIVE.
RECEPTIVE, BUT ASSERTIVE.
(30.06.2024)

We build walls around our hearts, hoping it protects us from pain and suffering, from bad actors with bad intentions. It is a fool's errand, of course. Heartbreak is always an inside job. We, the ones with the closed hearts, hiding our scars, are the bad actors. If we don't show our true selves to the world, why would the world reflect anything true back to us? If there is a wounded, disappointed, fearful little boy or girl inside of you, who hasn't been given the chance to grow up, then the world will treat you as such. Tear down the wall. It may be painful, but it is true. Behind the wall is the truth about your nature. If you truly accept that as an integral part of you, then so will the world accept that; and align you with what is really meant for you.

(18.11.2024)

18. On Time

THE MOST IMPORTANT THING THE
CURRENT SYSTEM ROBS FROM US IS
TIME. TIME IS SUCH A POWERFUL
ENERGY, AND IT IS ALSO RELENTLESS.
THE DUALITY OF LIFE PRESENTS ITSELF
HERE AS WELL: TIME IS BOTH OUR BEST
FRIEND AND BIGGEST ENEMY.

(21.03.2023)

BAD THINGS TEND TO MANIFEST
QUICKLY SO YOU COULD LEARN FROM
THEM.

GOOD THINGS TEND TO MANIFEST
SLOWLY BECAUSE YOU HAVE TO EARN
THEM.

(28.04.2023)

THE PAST BELONGS TO DEATH;
THE FUTURE BELONGS
TO THE UNIVERSE;
ALL WE HAVE IS NOW.
(05.10.2023)

DON'T LIVE IN THE PAST,
THE FUTURE,
OR THE FANTASIES.
LIVE ONLY IN THE NOW.
(19.10.2023)

19. Tongue-In-Cheek

TL;DR of The Basics of Yoga:

Fun

Sacrifice

???

Profit

(12.02.2023)

"Conspiracy theory" seems like a redundant term nowadays. "Conspiracy practice" seems more apt.

(12.02.2023)

What really concerns me is this: If I can't get a girlfriend, what hope do the rest of you poor sacks of shit have?

(14.02.2023)

I DON'T DO THIS TO "TEACH" ANYONE.
I DO THIS TO LATER POINT BACK AT IT
AND SAY: "I TOLD YOU SO."
DON'T MISTAKE MY VANITY
FOR CHARITY.
(17.02.2023)

I GUESS ONE WAY OF MAKING YOURSELF
RESISTANT TO LOSING EVERYTHING IS
TO NOT HAVE ANYTHING TO LOSE
IN THE FIRST PLACE.
(13.03.2023)

TEACH A MAN TO USE A GPS
AND HE'LL NEVER FIND HIS WAY
WITHOUT ONE AGAIN.
(19.03.2023)

TRY TO FIND OUT IF SHE CAN MAKE
POACHED EGGS.
IF SHE CAN MAKE POACHED EGGS,
SHE'S PROBABLY THE ONE.
(12.06.2023)

PERPETUALLY STUCK SOMEWHERE
BETWEEN GRATEFUL AND ANNOYED.
(19/22.08.2023)

I HATE IT WHEN PEOPLE ASK ME
STUPID SHIT LIKE
"DO YOU EVEN KNOW
WHAT YOU'RE DOING?"
IT'S LIKE, COME ON.
WHO DO YOU THINK I AM?
OF COURSE I DON'T KNOW WHAT I'M
DOING, THAT'S THE WHOLE POINT OF
DOING IT!
(05.10.2023)

WHEN YOU REALLY COME DOWN TO IT,
EVERYTHING IS A REMIX.
(18.10.2023)

OH, I HAVE A LOT OF FRIENDS. MANY
FANS. HORDES OF WOMEN MADLY IN
LOVE WITH ME. ADMIRERS, CUSTOMERS,
SUPPORTERS, COLLABORATORS,
BROTHERS IN ARMS, ETC. MOST OF
THEM JUST DON'T KNOW IT YET.
(20.10.2023)

IN ORDER TO DISTRACT MYSELF FROM
OVERTHINKING A PARTICULAR SUBJECT,
I WILL OVERTHINK THIS OTHER SUBJECT
INSTEAD.
(17.12.2023)

DON'T WORRY. YOU WILL DO TERRIBLY
IN LOVE. BUT AT LEAST YOU WILL BE BAD
IN BUSINESS AS WELL.
(06.01.2024)

DOGS ARE REALLY JUST WOLVES
WITH STOCKHOLM SYNDROME.
(11.01.2024)

I'M TAKING "BEING KIND TO YOURSELF"
TO A WHOLE NEW LEVEL.
I JUST THANKED MYSELF
FOR OPENING THE DOOR FOR ME.
(21.01.2024)

THE SITUATION IS EVEN WORSE
THAN I THOUGHT.
LET THAT BE A LESSON
NOT TO FUCKING THINK TOO MUCH.
(15.02.2024)

I LIKE TO ASK THE FIAT PEOPLE IN MY
LIFE FOR ADVICE AND THEN DO THE
EXACT OPPOSITE. IT'S LIKE THE INVERSE
CRAMER INDICATOR - ALMOST NEVER
FAILS. THE SAME LOGIC APPLIES WHEN
DEALING WITH ADVICE GIVEN BY YOUR
GOVERNMENT.
(17.02.2024)

PRO TIP: NEVER EVER TRY TO SAVE
MONEY ON SOMETHING AS ESSENTIAL AS
A JOURNAL. BECAUSE AN UGLY JOURNAL
IS LIKE AN UGLY SPOUSE -
NOT PARTICULARLY EXCITING.
(22.02.2024)

ALL I REALLY NEED
IS A '53 BEL AIR
AND A '53 AUDREY HEPBURN
(10.03.2024)

JUST IN CASE ANYBODY'S INTERESTED,

HERE'S MY SELF-CARE ROUTINE:

1. **BATHE IN THE TEARS OF MY ENEMIES**

AMAZING RESULTS SO FAR,

WOULD HIGHLY RECOMMEND.

(19.03.2024)

MEN DO THINGS NOT BECAUSE

THEY ARE EASY,

BUT BECAUSE THEY THINK

THEY ARE EASY.

(29.03.2024)

I MAY BE RETARDED,

BUT AT LEAST I'M NOT STUPID ENOUGH

TO FALL FOR THE GOVERNMENT

PROPAGANDA.

(19.05.2024)

SOME OF YOU MOTHERFUCKERS
NEVER EXPERIENCED EGO DEATH
AND IT SHOWS.
(19.05.2024)

SOME OF YOU MOTHERFUCKERS
NEVER READ "MEDITATIONS"
BY MARCUS AURELIUS
AND IT SHOWS.
(27.05.2024)

IF THE SITUATION IS BAD RIGHT NOW,
DON'T WORRY;
IT CAN ALWAYS GET WORSE.
(20.07.2024)

20. Common Sense

DON'T INVENT THE BICYCLE.

JUST RIDE IT.

(25.12.2022)

IF YOUR INTELLIGENCE CAN BE
INSULTED...

IS IT REALLY EVEN INTELLIGENCE?

(14.06.2023)

DON'T ASSUME, VERIFY.

(08.11.2023)

I SEE NO REASON TO WORRY ABOUT
ANYTHING THAT IS NOT UNDER MY
CONTROL.

(20.01.2024)

HOW DO YOU JUDGE A PHILOSOPHY?
BY THE QUALITY OF THE PEOPLE
WHO LIVE BY IT.
(16.04.2024)

YELLING AT A PROBLEM
WON'T MAKE IT GO AWAY.
(29.05.2024)

BREAKING THE RULES HAS ITS
CONSEQUENCES.
ESPECIALLY BREAKING YOUR OWN RULES.
(04.10.2024)

21. On Truth

PREDICTING AND MANIFESTING ARE THE
SAME THING. ONCE YOU SEE THE TRUTH,
PREDICTING BECOMES EASY. ONCE YOU
CAN EASILY PREDICT THINGS, YOU CAN
EITHER:

A) CHANGE THEM

OR

B) FIND A WAY TO USE THEM TO YOUR
ADVANTAGE

(19.03.2023)

IF YOU TRY TO CONVEY TRUTH OR
DISCIPLINE THROUGH A SYSTEM OF
RULES, YOU'RE ONLY GOING TO BUILD
RESISTANCE AND THUS THERE WILL BE
ENERGY LOSS.

(20.03.2023)

EVERYTHING YOU EXPERIENCE, YOU
EXPERIENCE ONLY FOR THE CHANCE TO
UNDERSTAND THE TRUE NATURE OF
REALITY, OF YOURSELF.

IF YOU DON'T TAKE THE CHANCE TO
LEARN, YOU WILL EXPERIENCE THESE
THINGS AGAIN, PERHAPS IN A SLIGHTLY
DIFFERENT FORM.

(23.03.2023)

WE'VE CONVERTED STORIES
INTO STORAGE.

(01.05.2023)

NOT SAYING THE TRUTH
WHEN IT NEEDS TO BE SAID
IS ALSO A FORM OF DISHONESTY.

(04.05.2023)

MOST "EXPERTS" ARE JUST THAT. THEY
ARE EXPERTS ON PAPER. EXPERTS IN
THEORY. AND LITERALLY, EXPERTS IN
THEORY. THE GUY OR THE LADY AT THE
BANK WHO'S IN CHARGE OF DECIDING
WHO GETS A BUSINESS LOAN AND WHO
DOESN'T, 9 TIMES OUT OF 10, HAS NEVER
RUN A BUSINESS THEMSELVES.
(12.05.2023)

IS YOUR OPINION THE TRUTH? NO.
IS YOUR PERCEPTION THE TRUTH? NO.
THEN WHY DO YOU TREAT THEM
AS IF THEY WERE?
(21.05.2023)

JUST BECAUSE IT'S LEGAL
DOESN'T MEAN IT'S MORAL.
JUST BECAUSE IT'S MORAL
DOESN'T MEAN IT'S LEGAL.
THAT'S A PROBLEM.
(26.05.2023)

THROUGH FIGURING OUT WHAT IT
ISN'T YOU CAN GET CLOSER
TO WHAT IT IS.
IT'S ALL GOOD.
(03.06.2023)

IF YOU ARE NOT READY TO BE PROVEN
WRONG THEN YOU ARE READY TO BE
DELUSIONAL.
(23.06.2023)

ANY TIME YOU ARE WRONG, AND ADMIT
YOU ARE WRONG, YOU GET CLOSER TO
THE TRUTH. DON'T BE AFRAID TO BE
WRONG. TAKE A CHANCE.
SOONER OR LATER, YOU WILL BE RIGHT.
(26.07.2023)

THE MESSENGERS WILL LIKELY BE SHOT
OR SHOT AT. THAT'S A RISK WE'RE
GOING TO HAVE TO TAKE.
(23.02.2024)

THERE ARE NO WHITE LIES.
THERE ARE ONLY GREY LIES
AND BLACK LIES.
(12.03.2024)

I WOULD RATHER DIE BY THE TRUTH
THAN LIVE BY A LIE
(29.03.2024)

WHEN THE TRUTH BECOMES
UNCOMFORTABLE, MOST PEOPLE REVERT
TO PERPETRATING THE ILLUSION.
THAT IS SOMETHING THAT YOU, AS AN
HONEST AND HONORABLE PERSON,
CANNOT AFFORD.
(28.04.2024)

I DON'T CARE ABOUT BEING "RIGHT"
I ONLY CARE ABOUT THE TRUTH
(22.05.2024)

Should I be worried if my ideas are wildly unpopular?
If I cared deeply about fame, money, and social status – yes.
But as I am only concerned with the truth, then no, I am perfectly fine with being right
while everyone else is wrong.
(19.06.2024)

The illusion of choice only presents itself to a person whose mind is uncertain, clouded, hesitant. He who has gone through the individuation process, who has truly found themselves, has no real, difficult choices. The path is laid before him, the destination is all but determined, and he knows that all he can really do is to simply walk the path.
(05.09.2024)

OH, I COULD PRETEND I'M NORMAL.

I COULD.

IT'S JUST... I'D RATHER NOT.

I'D RATHER NOT PRETEND ANYTHING.

(22.10.2024)

22. On Healing

The process of healing is primarily
a process of cleansing.
It's rarely pretty.
(25.03.2023)

What doesn't kill you
leaves you scarred for life
and creates mental blocks
regarding certain people
and situations.
The scars are fine,
the blockages must be dealt with.
(07.04.2023)

HERE'S THE THING ABOUT WEED. I'M A HIGHLY SENSITIVE PERSON. ALWAYS HAVE BEEN. BUT THERE'S A FINE LINE BETWEEN SENSITIVITY AND EMOTIONALITY. CANNABIS HELPS ME CONTROL MY EMOTIONALITY WHILE NOT DECREASING, BUT IN MOST INSTANCES EVEN INCREASING SENSITIVITY. THE THING WITH ALCOHOL, ON THE OTHER HAND, IS THE OPPOSITE. IT DECREASES YOUR SENSITIVITY WHILE INCREASING EMOTIONALITY.

(21.05.2023)

YES, IT IS

"FIX THE MONEY FIX THE WORLD" AND BITCOIN DOES FIX THE MONEY. HOWEVER, BEFORE WE CAN LET BITCOIN FIX THE WORLD, WE HAVE TO LET IT FIX **US.** YOUR FIAT SELF MUST DIE IN ORDER FOR YOUR TRUE SELF TO EMERGE.

(31.05.2023)

THERE WILL NOT BE A CHANGE
IN THE POLITICAL SYSTEM UNTIL WE
BYPASS THE POLITICAL SYSTEM.
(24.06.2023)

I THINK IT WOULD BE FAIR TO SAY THAT
THE SELF-DESTRUCTION OF THE
MILITARY-INDUSTRIAL COMPLEX BEGAN
WHEN THEY STARTED THEIR RESEARCH
ON CRYPTOGRAPHY AND PSYCHEDELICS.
PERHAPS IT WILL END WITH
HYPERBITCOINIZATION AND
WORLDWIDE LEGALIZATION OF
PSYCHEDELICS.
(24/25.06.2023)

NOBODY CAN SAVE ANYBODY
BUT THEMSELVES.
(25.06.2023)

THE GIST OF THE SITUATION:
EVERYBODY'S COMPROMISED.
SINCE THE INSTITUTIONS ARE
COMPROMISED, AND THE CONSTRUCTS
ARE COMPROMISED, AND THAT BOTH
INSTITUTIONS AND CONSTRUCTS ARE
COMPRISED OF INDIVIDUALS...
THEN INDIVIDUALS, TOO, ARE
INVARIABLY COMPROMISED
TO VARYING DEGREES.
(28.06.2023)

YOU DON'T REALLY WANT TO KNOW
WHETHER WHAT YOU'RE DOING IS
GOOD OR BAD, DO YOU? YOU ARE
CONSTANTLY SEEKING FOR ASSURANCE,
FOR VALIDATION, THAT IT IS, IN FACT,
GOOD WHAT YOU'RE DOING. THAT IS
VASTLY DIFFERENT FROM SEEKING THE
TRUTH. AND TO REALLY EVOLVE, IT'S THE
OPPOSITE, IT'S THE DARK, THE BAD
THINGS YOU NEED TO FIND AND SOLVE.

OTHERWISE YOU CAN KEEP LYING TO
YOURSELF, ONLY LOOK FOR VALIDATION,
AND PERHAPS CONSIDER OTHER
OPTIONS ONLY WHEN IT HURTS. AND
USUALLY ONCE ONE GOES DOWN THAT
PATH OF SELF-DECEPTION, THEY DON'T
REALIZE IT UNTIL IT HURTS REALLY
FUCKING BAD, BECAUSE WHAT DO YOU
KNOW, WE HAVE A WHOLE BUNCH OF
METHODS, CHEMICALS, ILLUSIONS TO
SUBSCRIBE TO, TO SUPPRESS THAT PAIN
TILL THE VERY END. THE "END" COMES
WHEN IT IS NO LONGER AN OPTION TO
SUPPRESS THE PAIN. THE "END" IS THE
BEGINNING OF THE SENSATION OF PAIN
AND IT MUST BE LIVED THROUGH. IT
MUST BE FULLY DEALT WITH FOR THE
"END" TO TRULY END.

(29.06.2023)

EVERYBODY'S A HEALER. BUT FIRST,
EVERYBODY MUST HEAL THEMSELVES.

(11.11.2023)

Saving the world is really easy.
It's literally just 2 steps:
1. Save yourself
2. Have lots of babies
(25.02.2024)

Mindset is very important.
No, mindset is everything.
(06.09.2024)

Only after acknowledging
my faults can I proceed
to fixing them.
(21.09.2024)

Mantras & Affirmations

I DO EVERYTHING WITH FULL TRUST
IN MY OWN INTUITION,
DRIVEN BY THE IDEALS OF
LOVE AND FREEDOM.

THERE MUST BE NO FEAR.
THERE MUST ONLY BE LOVE.

I AM NOT ENTITLED TO ANYTHING
AND
I AM GRATEFUL FOR EVERYTHING.

IF YOU FEEL LIKE SLIPPING.
COMPOSURE.
IF YOU FEEL LIKE LOSING CONTROL.
COMPOSURE.
ONE WORD.
COMPOSURE.
YOU CHOOSE WHO YOU ARE.

I AM ONE OF THE GUARDIANS OF LIFE.

TODAY IS THE LAST DAY
OF THE UNIVERSE. MAKE IT COUNT.
&
TODAY IS THE FIRST DAY
OF THE UNIVERSE. MAKE IT COUNT.

EVERYTHING I DO, I DO FOR YOU.
EVERYTHING I AM, I AM FOR YOU.
IF I'M STILL ALIVE, I'M ALIVE FOR YOU.

I WILL NOT JUDGE. I WILL NOT BE
AFRAID OF BEING JUDGED.

WHEN I GO TO SLEEP I DIE,
ONLY TO BE REBORN AGAIN
IN THE MORNING, A BETTER MAN